# ORAL LITERATURE

## Seven Essays

EDITED BY

## JOSEPH J. DUGGAN

BOOKS
10 East 53d St., New York 10022
(a division of Harper & Row Publishers, Inc.)

Published in the U.S.A. by
HARPER & ROW PUBLISHERS, INC.
BARNES & NOBLE IMPORT DIVISION


ISBN 0 06 491819 X

This edition first published 1975

Printed in Great Britain by
W. C. Henderson & Son Ltd., St. Andrews

# ORAL LITERATURE

# FOREWORD

In the 46 years which have passed since Milman Parry developed the theory of oral composition in order to explain the peculiarities of Homeric diction, his ideas have been adopted by scholars studying the medieval and modern literatures of Europe. The seven studies presented here cover topics ranging in chronology from the eighth to the nineteenth centuries. Although epic poetry was Parry's principal concern, the hymn, the saga, the romance, the novel of chivalry, and the drama are also represented in this collection.

Albert B. Lord surveys recent studies of oral literature composed in Ancient Greek, Old French, and Old English as well as in other languages, presenting his views on, among other matters, the possibility of identifying texts transitional between oral tradition and creation in writing, a question which has given rise to considerable controversy. Daniel F. Melia argues that at least one section of the *Cattle-Raid of Cooley*, " The Boyhood Deads of Cuchulainn ", contains independent, orally transmitted variants of an ancient theme which lead him to posit the existence of a living saga tradition in Ireland perhaps as late as the eleventh century. Donald K. Fry, after re-examining Bede's tale of how Caedmon began to sing, analyses his hymn into formulaic systems which the singer would have absorbed from listening to them—or to analogous systems—in the secular poetry of his day. Transformations in the audience's mode of perceiving the *Nibelungenlied* as it moved from oral tradition to the more static existence of a written artifact are the concern of Franz H. Bäuml and Edda Spielmann. In the context of statistics gathered for a study of formulas in the *chanson de geste*, Joseph J. Duggan concludes that the *Cantar de mio Cid* bears a quantitative formulaic profile which is typical of orally-composed epics. L. P. Harvey's case history of the Morisco story-teller Román Ramirez, charged by the Inquisition with acts of witchcraft which included the recitation of novels of chivalry from memory, provides a well-documented Spanish counterpart to the example of Caedmon. Finally, Elizabeth A. Warner shows how, in more recent times, elements from Pushkin's poems have been incorporated into the orally transmitted Russian folk-plays and suffered some curious distortion in the process.

The interests and approaches of these eight scholars—textual criticism, historical documentation, the analysis of diction, the theory of oral poetry, and the exploration of oral literature's function in society—are a fair representation of the diversity of studies now being carried out on in this field.

J. J. D.

# CONTRIBUTORS

ALBERT B. LORD is Professor of Slavic and Comparative Literature and Honorary Curator of the Milman Parry Collection at Harvard University. He is the author of *The Singer of Tales*, *Serbo-Croatian Folk Songs* (with Béla Bartók), *Serbo-Croatian Heroic Songs*, and various studies on the theory of oral poetry and on Greek and Serbo-Croatian epic.

DANIEL F. MELIA, Assistant Professor of Rhetoric at the University of California, Berkeley, is working on a book on narrative structures in the Irish saga.

DONALD K. FRY is Professor of English at the University of the State of New York, Stony Brook. He has devoted numerous studies to formulas, themes, and type-scenes in Old English poetry.

FRANZ H. BÄUML, Professor of German at the University of California, Los Angeles, has written *Medieval Civilization in Germany: 800-1273*, *Rhetorical Devices and Structure in the Ackermann aus Bohmen*, and *Kudrun: die Handschrift*. About to appear are *A Dictionary of Gestures* and *A Concordance to the Nibelungenlied*.

EDDA SPIELMANN, Assistant Professor of German at California State University, Northridge, has written on *Yvain* and is working on an analysis of the prologue to Hartmann von Aue's *Iwein*.

JOSEPH J. DUGGAN, Associate Professor of French and Comparative Literature at the University of California, Berkeley, is the author of *The Song of Roland: Formulaic Style and Poetic Craft* and *A Concordance of the Chanson de Roland*. He is now working on the troubadour William IX of Aquitaine.

L. P. HARVEY, Professor of Spanish at King's College, London, has published widely on the relations between Arabic and Spanish literatures in the Middle Ages.

ELIZABETH A. WARNER is a Lecturer in Russian language and literature at the University of Hull. Her main research interest is Russian folklore, in particular the folk theatre, and she has written a number of articles on this subject, as well as *The Russian Folk Theatre* (in preparation, Mouton, The Hague). She is currently interested in children's games and creatures from Russian mythology.

# CONTENTS

# PERSPECTIVES

# ON

# RECENT WORK ON ORAL LITERATURE

During the last ten or fifteen years the study of oral literature has been enriched by many books and articles representing research and criticism in a wide variety of fields. The recently published *Haymes Bibliography of the Oral Theory*, Publications of the Milman Parry Collection, (Cambridge, Mass., 1973) is a most welcome guide and *sine qua non*, yet already a supplement is being prepared for the numerous works that have appeared later or that its compiler and editors have since discovered or had brought to their attention. Generally speaking, while comparatively little work has been done on analysis of living oral tradition, much has been written on applying oral theory to ancient and medieval texts. The application has outdistanced the new presentation of an exact description of an oral traditional poetry. I say new, because we tend to forget that before Parry's time at least three oral poetries had been well described. There was W. Radloff's classic description of Turkish epic songs (*Proben der Volkslitteratur der nördlichen Türkischen Stämme*, V, St Petersburg, 1885), D. Comparettie's book on the Finnish *Kalevala* (Domenico Comparetti, *The Traditional Poetry of the Finns* (London, 1898): the Italian original was published in Rome in 1891, *Il Kalevala o la poesia tradizionale dei Finni*), and the several collections of Russian epic songs, such as those of Hilferding and Rybnikov (A. F. Hilferding, *Onežskija byliny*, St Petersburg, 1873 ; P. N. Rybnikov, *Pjesni*, 4 volumes, Moscow and St Petersburg, 1861-1867), with descriptions of singers and singing, including versions of songs from a number of singers.

These collections still merit our attention. We are extremely fortunate to have F. P. Magoun Jr.'s recent translations of the *Kalevala* (1963) and of the *Old Kalevala* (1969) and pertinent material, both publications of the Harvard University Press. We still need English translations of the Turkish and Russian songs.

Aside from a small number of articles, the first main step in this century in describing an oral lyric and epic tradition with as great accuracy as modern methods of collecting can afford was Milman Parry's collection of South Slavic songs, the publication of which began with *Serbo-Croatian Folk Songs* (Columbia University Press, 1951) by Bela Bartók and Albert B. Lord, and continued in 1953-54 with volumes I and II of *Serbo-Croatian Heroic Songs* (Harvard University Press). Here were presented real oral traditional texts without editorial changes, a microcosm of an oral tradition. The seeds of the answers to most of the questions of scholars were, and are, at hand in those volumes. The results of my own research on Serbo-Croatian poetry appeared in 1960 in *The Singer of Tales* (Harvard U.P.). It set forth the processes of composition and transmission of that oral traditional poetry. The scene was thus nearly all set for the next act in this scholarly drama. The first volumes of *Serbo-Croatian Heroic Songs* had provided textual materials and *The Singer of Tales* had presented the description of the processes. There was, however, one major piece of evidence still lacking. When it was forthcoming, all else would, hopefully, be modification, improvement, refinement. The missing publication was that of one of the long songs of Avdo Medjedović, "The Wedding of Smailagić Meho," and it is now in press.

There has, as I have said, been comparatively little published recently presenting the results of study and analysis of living oral traditions, but there is an encouraging amount of work completed, but not yet published, or now in progress. The study of formulaic structure and thematic composition in the Slavic poetries has on the whole taken strong root in the Slavic countries themselves. Slavic scholars abroad are more concerned with history than with style. The publications of the late Alois Schmaus of Munich on the South Slavic poetries, both Serbo-Croatian and Bulgarian, form an exception, as did the earlier articles of Gerhard Gesemann. Gesemann's study of " schemata " in the Serbo-Croatian songs was a forerunner of Parry's thematic investigations, and Schmaus's *Studije o krajinskoj epici* (Studies of the epics of the Krajina), Zagreb, 1953, is one of the very few books devoted to the Moslem epics of northern Bosnia and their style.

What has been done more recently in the Slavic field, insofar as I know, has been done in this country, mostly at Harvard due to the impetus of the Milman Parry Collection. The first doctoral dissertation at Harvard (after my own in 1949) to make use of the texts of the Milman Parry Collection was that of Eugene E. Pantzer, which was summarized later in an article "Yugoslav Epic Preambles", *Slavic and East European Journal* 17 (1959), 372-381. Professor Patricia Arant of Brown University in her doctoral dissertation at Harvard made a formulaic and thematic analysis of some of the Russian *byliny* about Dobrynja, " Compositional Techniques of the Russian Oral Epic, the Bylina " (1963), and she has been working more recently on Russian laments. Her analyses were among the first to demonstrate the effectiveness of Parry's techniques on another living oral tradition. Dr David E. Bynum, Curator of the Milman Parry Collection, in his doctoral dissertation at Harvard (1964) under the title " A Taxonomy of Oral Narrative Song: The Isolation and Description of Invariables in Serbocroatian Tradition," investigated thematic structure in a large selection of songs of weddings, and his book on thematics, now in the last stages of preparation, will present a new approach to that subject. He has also contributed to Homeric scholarship in a noteworthy article, " Themes of the Young Hero in Serbocroatian Oral Epic Tradition" (*PMLA* 83 (1968), 1296-1303), in which he uses the Slavic evidence for an interpretation of Telemachus in the *Odyssey*. He has also prepared the text of " The Wedding of Smailagić Meho " for publication, as well as two forthcoming volumes in the *Serbo-Croatian Heroic Songs* series, including selected texts from northern Bosnia together with translations and commentary.

Professor John Kolsti (University of Texas, Austin) wrote his Harvard dissertation on one of the Parry Collection's bilingual singers in Novi Pazar, who sang in both Serbo-Croatian and Albanian. He analyzed both formulas and themes and noted the correspondences between formulas in Serbo-Croatian and Albanian. He has also prepared Albanian texts collected by myself in 1937 for publication together with translations. Finally, Mrs Mary Coote (University of California, Berkeley) in her thesis at Harvard dealt with the songs of another Parry Collection singer, this one from northern Bosnia, analyzing the content of his themes, and his use of them in making songs.

Two dissertations using texts from the Milman Parry Collection at Harvard are now in progress. Kenneth Goldman has put eight songs from a singer in Hercegovina onto the computer, and the print-outs, following the method of Professor Duggan at Berkeley for the *chansons de geste*, are being used for a study of that singer's formula habits. With it, for the first time, we shall have formulaic analysis of whole songs in a living oral tradition. This technique should be extended to other singers and to whole regions in order that we might be able to speak with exactness about formulas in the habits of individuals in relationship to one another in a singing group, as well as between regions. Miss Laura Gordon is writing an evaluation of the songs of Marko Kraljević in the Parry Collection. In her thesis she is comparing the unpublished songs collected in the thirties and later with those in the collections published in the nineteenth century.

The late Professor James A. Notopoulos of Trinity College, Hartford, Connecticut, has a special place in the register of those who have collected and studied living oral literary traditions. A Greek scholar, whose writings early made significant contributions to Homeric and Hesiodic studies (especially "Parataxis in Homer", *TAPA* 80 (1949), 1-23, "The Generic and Oral Composition in Homer", *TAPA* 81 (1950), 28-36, and "Continuity and Interconnexion in Homeric Oral Composition", *TAPA* 82 (1951), 81-101) Notopoulos made his own collections in 1953-54 of Greek ballads and lyrics in many parts of Greece and the islands. His collection was bequeathed to Harvard University and is now housed, together with the Parry Collection, in Widener Library. He left a manuscript of a book on Cretan Heroic Song and Homer, which is presently being edited.

The work of all these scholars has added, and is continuing to add much to our knowledge of how a living tradition of oral epic functions. Our main problem is to see that the information gained in this research be published and brought to the attention of scholars working in other areas who need to know as exactly as possible what an oral tradition of narrative song is like. In all but one of the above cases the tradition concerned is South Slavonic (or Albanian). We need more researchers to follow the path opened up by Professor Arant in her study of the Russian songs and to extend it to include Ukrainian. We would then have an invaluable total picture of the stylistics of the great Slavic branch of the Indo-European peoples. An important beginning has been made, and the necessary materials are available. We need to compare the techniques in the three divisions of the Slavs who have, or have had, an oral epic tradition.

Some investigation has been made of living oral traditions outside Europe and Slavic Russia. One of the questions which comes to our minds is whether the processes of which we speak are peculiar to Indo-European, or more particularly Slavic, traditions. We know that oral poetries exist elsewhere. Do they follow the same laws of composition and transmission?

Although the late Viktor Žirmunskij and others have given us excellent descriptions of Central Asiatic epic, which are very useful for studies of a comparative nature, especially in respect to details of subject and structure of the songs, no formulaic or thematic study of that material has, to the best of my knowledge, appeared. The chant-fable tradition among the Turkic peoples is worthy of special interest. At present, however, Mrs Natalie Moyle at Harvard is preparing such a study of several Turkish minstrel tales which she has herself collected in Turkey, together with others in private collections in this country. Repetition has been pointed out as one of the characteristics of Central Asiatic narrative poetry, and examples have been cited, but no detailed investigation has been made before this. At the present time, there are also two graduate students at Harvard, Miss Margaret Mills and Mrs Mahasti Ziai, working on Persian epic, and their dissertations should add to our knowledge in this significant area, where we have not only older material in the *Shahname*, but there is also a living tradition of narrative song to be collected and studied. Finally, from India comes a book by K. Kailasapathy, *Tamil Heroic Poetry* (Oxford,

1968), giving a full description and analysis of the songs of those peoples, which combines the approach of the Heroic Age as set forth by the Chadwicks with Milman Parry's analysis of formula style and thematic composition.

Ruth Finnegan's book on *African Oral Literature* brought attention to an area which, like Central Asia, is rich in possibilities. Hers is a survey, a much needed overview, replacing the Chadwicks' previous summary with something more immediate and substantial. In the same Oxford series in which her book appeared, Professor Daniel Kunene in his *Heroic Poetry of the Basotho* (1971) has written a detailed and sensitive account of his subject. Kunene does not follow the formulaic and thematic type of analysis associated with Milman Parry, although he is well acquainted with it, but makes his own kind of investigation. This is perhaps as well, because the heroic poetry with which he is dealing is not narrative in our sense of the word, but eulogistic ; it is praise poetry of a kind common, I believe, in Africa. Kunene's work adds a new dimension to the study of oral literature which is most welcome and deserves to be much better known than it is to all scholars in the field. Professor Jeffrey Opland of the University of Durban, South Africa, who has previously published " The Oral Origins of Early English Poetry " in the *University of Cape Town Studies in English* (1970) has done field work and collected among the Xhosa peoples, and has an article forthcoming on their practice of oral poetic composition, its several kinds, improvised and memorised, amateur and professional. Mrs Marion Wilson of Simmons College has made an important study of songs she collected in Ghana in 1964-65, *Kpele Lala, Ga Religious Songs and Symbols* (Harvard U.P., 1971). She concerns herself with many aspects of the songs, their function in the community, their world view, and also their structure, including forms of variation and repetition. I understand that she has collected material from the Mende in Sierra Leone and is now at work on a book of their oral literature. Finally, Mr Clement Okafor of Nigeria is presently writing a doctoral dissertation at Harvard with Dr David Bynum, analysing the style of Tonga texts that he himself taped in the field a few years ago.

There is, I am sure, other research recently published, or now going on, of which I do not know, but the above examples indicate clearly that in the last few years attention has been turning to the oral literature of living traditions, not only in the Balkans and in the Slavic countries, but also in Asia and Africa. In all these areas more needs to be done. Where collections exist they need to be published and studied ; new collections must be made in those regions where there has not been sufficient field work. The texts must be viewed from all aspects, not only that of stylistics but also of sociology, religion, and history, so that a concept of oral literature's place in the whole society may be properly understood. The work now going on gives one hope for the future.

Of the older literatures, ancient or medieval, that have been approached as oral, or possibly oral, three have been the focus of most of the writing before the nineteen sixties: Ancient Greek, Old English, and Old French. In the last fifteen years research of this kind has been extended to a number of other literatures, and this has been a significant trend. A few examples will illustrate this important development.

The Ancient Near East is represented by the as yet unpublished Harvard dissertation of Professor Richard E. Whitaker, *A Formulaic Analysis of Ugaritic Poetry* (1969). Dr Whitaker analysed the formulas in his material with the help of the computer, and it is to be hoped that both his thesis and his computer print-outs will be published. He is now in the Near East collecting poetry with a tape recorder in the same geographic area from which the Ugaritic poetry from the past has come. The only work I know that deals with Sumerian texts as oral literature is Bendt Alster's *Dumuzi's Dream, Aspects of Oral Poetry in a Sumerian Myth* (Copenhagen, 1972). His work was encouraged by Professors Thorkild Jacobsen and W. Moran at Harvard, and Dr Whitaker's thesis was prepared under the direction of Professor Frank M. Cross, Jr. A slightly older work than the above two is that of Robert C. Culley, *Oral Formulaic Language in the Biblical Psalms*, (Toronto, 1967) which. as the author tells us in his preface, stemmed indirectly from Professor J. B. Bessinger's seminar on Old English.

Dr Ching-Hsien Wang's book on Chinese lyrical poetry is of special value because it applies formulaic and thematic analysis, modified for the Chinese language, to lyrical rather than epic poetry. Under the title " Shi Ching: Formulaic Language and Mode of Creation " it will soon be published by the University of California Press at Berkeley. The poems of the classical *Shih Ching* are very ancient, dating from before Confucius (550-479 B.C.) and Dr Wang's formulaic and thematic study of them is most illuminating. Dr Alsace Chun-Ching Yen's doctoral dissertation at Harvard, "Demon Tales in Early Vernacular Chinese; A Folkloristic View " (1971), analysed formulas and themes in a well-known collection of Chinese stories of the supernatural from the fifteenth century, and he has followed it by several articles on Chinese folklore and oral theory.

Mrs Nabeneeta Sen of Jadavpur University, Calcutta, published her first article on the Sanskrit epic in 1966 in the Journal of the *American Oriental Society*, " Comparative Studies in Oral Epic Poetry and the *Valmiki Ramayana*: A Report on the *Balakanda* ", which included formula analyses of the now classic type. Her latest paper, " Thematic Structure of Epic Poems in the East and in the West, A Comparative Study ", was presented to the VIIth International Comparative Literature Association Conference in Montreal and Ottawa in 1973. Here also should be mentioned the recent dissertation of Dr Mary Carroll Smith at Harvard, " The Core of India's Great Epic " (1972).

In *The Singer of Tales* in 1960, I raised the question of formulas in the

Byzantine Greek epic of *Digenis Akritas* and indicated the possibility that the Escorialensis manuscript of the poem might contain an oral traditional text. Reservations about this were expressed by Agostino Pertusi of Rome in his paper at a conference on epic poetry held at the Accademia nazionale dei Lincei in 1969, " La poesia epica bizantina e la sua formazione: problemi sul fondo storico e las structura letteraria del Digenis Akritas ". It and another paper on the *Digenis Akritas* by Linos Politis, " L'épopée byzantine de Digenis Akritas. Problèmes de la tradition du texte et des rapports avec les chansons acritiques ", were published in the proceedings of the conference *La poesia epica e la sua formazione*, Accademia nazionale dei Lincei, quaterno 139, Roma, 1970. In an article, " Formulas in the Chronicle of the Morea " in *Dumbarton Oaks Papers*, 27 (1973), 163-195, Mr Michael J. Jeffreys has a formulaic analysis, made with the help of computers, of the *Chronicle of Morea*. This will be an important addition to our understanding of traditional forms in texts perhaps not traditional in character. He suggests that the linguistic mixture of ancient and modern forms in the text may have resulted from a long tradition of oral poems.

Dr Daniel Frederick Melia's dissertation at Harvard, " Narrative Structure in Irish Saga " (1972), has broken new ground in Old Irish studies, and is typical of pioneering work in Celtic scholarship in the field of oral literature. The reader can find out further about Dr Melia's work from his article in this volume. Mr Edgar Slotkin of the University of Cincinnati also writes on the subject of medieval Irish oral literature, analyzing formula structures and metrical frames in some of the older documents.

I hope that the preceding survey of some of the work that has recently been done and is now being done on oral literature, both in living traditions and in older texts outside of the central core of writings in Ancient Greek, Old French and Old English, will be some indication of the growth of scholarly interest in this subject.

Let me turn now to an overview of recent work in Ancient Greek, Old French, and Old English, because it is in these areas that most controversy has been engendered and most, though not by any means all, theoretical problems have been aired.

## ANCIENT GREEK

By and large, I believe it is true in Ancient Greek scholarship that Homer's place as an oral poet has been accepted, sometimes a bit grudgingly, and that Hesiod too, after the work of a series of careful scholars, has been accorded a place in oral tradition. In Hesiod's case the earlier writings of J. A. Notopoulos have been followed more recently by those of G. P. Edwards, A. Hoekstra, W. W. Minton, and most recently Berkeley Peabody. With the exception of Peabody's, much of the concern of scholars is with his relationship to the Homeric poems. It is usually assumed that Homer represents " the " tradition and that differences between Homer and Hesiod are departures, whether development or decline, from " the " tradition. One sees a Hesiod who knew the *Iliad* and the *Odyssey* and proceeded from them as the tradition. What seems to be lacking is a broader concept of oral tradition, such as, indeed, is reflected in an admirable recent article by Geoffrey Kirk, " The Search for the Real Homer ", *Greece and Rome*, Second Series, XX, No. 2, (October, 1973), 124-139. The Homeric poems are only two performances by a single singer, or by two different singers, in the ancient Greek tradition of narrative song. Homer in his lifetime performed many times over a long period of time not only those songs, if they are both his, but probably many others as well. There were other singers before him, contemporary with him, and after him, also with many performances of many songs. One must also take geographic range into consideration. The singers in the ancient Greek tradition were not all located in one town or city or region. Thus one must realize that if Homer and Hesiod were oral poets the differences between them, other than those connected with a difference of subject matter, may be simply those between individuals in different places as well as different times. From that point of view neither of them is more " the " tradition than the other. As Geoffrey Kirk's article indicates, a realization of this aspect of tradition is becoming clearer in Greek scholarship.

From the standpoint of oral literature the most difficult problem with Hesiod concerns the *Works and Days* rather than the *Theogony*. The latter is not an anomaly in an oral tradition. Songs of the gods and of the creation and ordering of the universe and the establishment of the base of power are common enough, and play a highly significant role in oral narrative traditions in many places. But what kind of song is the *Works and Days*? When would such a song be sung in a traditional society? With these questions, of course, are associated that of the unity of the composition. Is it a series of separate songs or a single one? If one accepts Hesiod as an oral traditional poet, then these questions clamor even more for an answer. In a book entitled " The Winged Word " soon to be published by the State University of New York at Albany Press, Professor Berkeley Peabody of that university has an ingenious answer to these questions. Part of the book deals with the history of the hexameter, and I shall return to that shortly, but part is concerned with a complicated, yet methodologically, I believe, quite correct analysis of the structure of the poem, which leaves one with a clear concept of a unified composition. By noting thematic and acoustic responsions and echoes that are characteristic of oral composition, Peabody leads the reader from the beginning of the *Works and Days* through to the end. I found it both an exciting and a convincing adventure. His suggestion about the kind of poem which the *Works and Days* is, or might be, is equally ingenious, if somewhat less convincing, although I believe it is the best so far ; namely, it is a song used, presumably by Hesiod, in a contest with another singer. I leave the argument for the reader of " The Winged Word " to follow, but

I might give a hint that the parallel situation is to be found in one of the songs of the *Kalevala* in which Väinäimöinen contests in song with a younger challenger Joukahäinen.

It is no easy task to assess Homeric scholarship at the present time, because there is so much of it and because of its variety. The late Adam Parry's Introduction to his edition of his father's works, *The Making of Homeric Verse* (Oxford U.P., 1971) is very useful for this purpose. Thanks to the astuteness of a number of scholars we know more about the Homeric formula and formula systems than ever before, and the hexameter has come under very careful and imaginative scrutiny. In these regards the work of J. B. Hainsworth, A. Hoekstra, Michael Nagler, Gregory Nagy, and Berkeley Peabody have been outstanding. We know the flexibility of the formula from Hainsworth and Hoekstra, and the latter has attempted to reconstruct an older layer of formulas, although this is a very difficult task and some may doubt his results. Nagler has led us into a more abstract realm along the lines of generative-transformational grammar ; his work is challenging, but I sometimes feel that the individual composing poet is lost in its rarified atmosphere. His most recent work soon to be published by the University of California Press at Berkeley I have not yet seen, but it promises to be an important contribution to Homeric scholarship. In short, the formulaic weave of Ancient Greek oral narrative song is emerging ever more clearly as the product of generations of singers who composed in it, as did Homer, with the ease that others compose the sentences and paragraphs of everyday speech.

The forthcoming books of Berkeley Peabody, of which I have already spoken, and of Professor Gregory Nagy deserve special mention when one turns to the hexameter. Nagy's book, " Comparative Studies in Greek and Indic Meter ", will soon appear in the Comparative Literature series published by Harvard University Press. Nagy centers his work on a single formula, *kleos andron*, found in Homer and Sappho, and its Sanskrit equivalent, from which he reconstructs an Indo-European formula. He is led thus to Greek lyric poetry as well as epic, and with the help of the Indic parallels derives the hexameter from a pherecratic with the internal expansion of three dactyls. Peabody, on the other hand, while also using the Indic parallels, makes larger use of the Avesta with the stanzaic form that it shares, in part at least, with Indic, and derives the hexameter from a fusion of a dimeter with a trimeter. He thus accounts for the various caesuras in the line differently from Nagy. I feel that both these books will be richly discussed ; for they both add much to our knowledge of the metrical context and depth of the Ancient Greek tradition.

In an appendix Nagy presents an explanation of the meaning of the word *kleos*. The argument is involved, and some scholars will surely disagree with it, but I note that both Peabody and Nagy conclude their extraordinarily fine books with a reference to the magic or sacred power of song. Nagy writes: " I propose, then, that *klewos was the word used to designate the hieratic art of song which ensured unfailing streams of water, light, vegetal sap, etc. Since these streams were unfailing, the art of song itself could be idealized and self-servingly glorified by the Singer as ' unfailing '."

Thus the search for special meaning and contextual relevance of formulas moves forward. A number of Nagy's students at Harvard have been working in this vineyard and several challenging doctoral dissertations have resulted. Here, too, special mention should be made of Professor William Whallon's book *Formula, Character, and Context, Studies in Homeric, Old English, and Old Testament Poetry*, Center for Hellenic Studies, 1969. In the first chapter he says that he simply wishes to discuss cases that Parry neglected to mention where " epithets describe the essential and unchanging character of the men whose names they augment ". His examples are worthy of attention, as are those in his second chapter on epithets and characterization. In short his book is a reasonable and moderate attempt to counteract what is often thought of as Parry's too mechanical explanation of epithets and other formulas, namely, their use for filling a line, or for fitting a given noun into a given metrical space. Once again, in closing this section, I would like to refer to Geoffrey Kirk's discussion of formulas in the article in *Greece and Rome* referred to above.

Although classicists and medievalists have not on the whole been inclined to use the Serbo-Croatian (or other oral traditional) materials themselves for comparative research, there are at least two studies of theme in Homer which have been introduced by an investigation of theme in *Serbocroatian Heroic Songs* and thus deserve special mention. William F. Hansen, Jr.'s doctoral dissertation at Berkeley in 1970, recently (1972) published, scrutinized *The Conference Sequence, Patterned Narration and Narrative Inconsistency in the Odyssey*. David M. Gunn of the University of Newcastle upon Tyne published an article in *Harvard Studies in Classical Philology*, 75 (1971) investigating "Thematic Composition and Homeric Authorship", in which he first looked at the same theme in the songs of several singers in *SCHS*, noting the individual differences. From a similar consideration of passages in the Homeric poems Gunn concluded that the two songs were indeed by the same singer. Although the investigation should be carried much further than Mr Gunn did in his article, the general method employed seems to me to be acceptable.

Other studies of themes in the Homeric poems include Joseph A. Russo's " Homer Against his Tradition ", *Arion* 7 (1968), 275-295, in which he attempts to see Homer's hand in the more elaborate forms of any given theme. He considers the short forms of a theme, such as that of arming, to be traditional, whereas the longer examples are Homer's own use of tradition. While there is something, to be sure, to be said for ascribing to Homer the fact of expansion of themes, it does not follow that the material used by him to expand is any less traditional than that in the unexpanded instances. G. S. Kirk's brief discussion of Homer's handling of traditional themes is more successful in " The Search for the Real Homer ", *Greece and Rome*, 2nd series, Vol. XX, No. 2 (October, 1973) 124-139. But the fullest study of any Homeric theme is that of Bernard Fenik, *Typical Battle Scenes in the Iliad, Studies in the Narrative Techniques of Homeric Battle Description, Hermes*, Einzelschriften Heft 21, Wiesbaden, 1968. This is a very fine and significant work, and I am tempted to quote a few sentences from his conclusion:

> " The technique of composing a battle scene was therefore related to that of composing a single phrase or line. The poet had certain ready-made compositional elements at his disposal ; dictional formula, formulaic lines, typical details, typical groupings of details, recurrent situations. He created his battle scenes out of pre-formed, standardized material that had been used before, probably by himself as well as by other poets . . . .
>
> Thus far there is no method to distinguish between the type scenes, patterns and all their particular variations which Homer may have invented himself, and those which he inherited from the tradition. It is, however, as unlikely that one man invented all the typical details and type scenes in the battle narrative as that one man created the formulaic diction of the Iliad and Odyssey. Both these stylistics features are at home only in a learned, inherited style —what we might call a stylistic tradition—formed and shared by many poets over many generations." (p. 229)

And from his introduction:

> " It has become fashionable in certain quarters to emphasize the atypical or unique features in the Iliad on the ground that this is, after all, where Homer's particular excellence lies. A study of Homer's poetic technique must have as its goal the discovery of his variations on formular material and the special effects that he achieves with them. Some eminently worth-while work has already been done along this line. An especially fine example is J. Armstrong's study of the arming scenes, in which he shows the effect that is achieved by a slight change in a typical arming sequence (" The Arming Motif in the Iliad ", *AJPh* 79 (1958), 337-354). But it is one thing to do this for a relatively small homogeneous group of scenes, and quite another to attempt it amid the welter of small incidents in the rest of the fighting. . . . We cannot pick out the unique element in a passage, the significant variation, unless we have some means of identifying it, and we can do this only if we have first established, at least so far as is possible, what is typical." (p. 8)

It would be less than fair of me not to quote something of Fenik's opinion about the orality of the Homeric poems and about the value of the comparison of compositional techniques in Homer and Serbo-Croatian oral narrative song:

> " The existence of a ' typical style ' of battle description has certain clear, but limited, implications for the theory of oral poetry. The nature of this style, like the nature of the diction, indicates that it was created under the pressure of oral recitation, in which the poet

had no time to stop and ponder each new phrase or each new incident
on the battlefield. But it does need to be emphasized that the typical
style of the battle scenes does not prove, any more than does the
formulaic language, that the Iliad is a purely oral composition. Only
that the diction and style of the poem grew out of an oral tradition
is certain. The exact nature of the poetic inheritance, the way it
was handed down, as well as the particular set of circumstances
which produced the Iliad still remain largely unclear." (229-230)

Finally, in speaking of the *Iliad* vis-a-vis the Serbo-Croatian songs Fenik
writes:

" The formidable differences between the poems imply equally considerable differences in the poetic traditions and specific circumstances
out of which they grew. The modern parallels doubtless illuminate a
great deal in the Homeric poems, and in this respect they are most
valuable, but they leave even more unexplained—particularly the
overwhelming excellence of the Iliad and Odyssey.

. . . for an outstanding poet to achieve anything approaching the
quality of a poem like the Iliad he must have had the benefit of a
tradition and training, in whatever form, far superior to anything
which prevails among, say, the Yugoslav oral poets today. Many
important pieces to the puzzle are still missing." (p. 230)

Fenik is not the only scholar, of course, who has found it difficult to see
the relevance of the Serbo-Croatian songs to Homer. Geoffrey Kirk's
reservations in this regard are well known and were voiced in *The Songs of
Homer* (1962) and elsewhere. They agree that the Serbo-Croatian tradition
can show us the importance of formulas and themes as the pragmatic basic
composition of oral story verse. I do not think that this much has really
ever been denied ; its validity is actually demonstrable. It was precisely in
order to learn something of the processes of composition and transmission
that the study of the living oral traditions of the Balkans was undertaken.
To this extent it can be said that the comparison with the Serbo-Croatian
material has already had an impact. The South Slavic singers have taught
us a great deal about the mechanics of oral composition of traditional narrative verse or song, and we should be willing to acknowledge, as Fenik has,
at least that much of a debt to them. To do otherwise would seem to me to
be unjust. They have, however, shown us more than the mechanics of the
style. We have been able to see in the modern Balkans the *whole* of a tradition and that over a long period of time—not just two songs from one
singer but many songs from many singers, some good, some mediocre, some
bad. We have seen young singers and old singers, and middle-aged singers.
The lesson for us in this is that we should realize that the Ancient Greek
tradition, if it was a real living dynamic organism, and the Homeric poems
prove that it certainly was just that, also had good, bad, and mediocre
singers, young, old and middle-aged singers in addition to Homer, and
probably some other superb singers, standing head and shoulders above even
the good ones.

As a matter of fact, we do not really have the means as objective scholars to judge Homer's relationship to his own tradition, because, except for the Hesiodic poems, which are on different subjects, even different kinds of subjects, we have no other poems from ancient Greece with which to compare them. We do the best we can with late summaries, with fragments, with whatever clues have survived, but our best evidence is Homer's reputation, the reverence with which he was treated. The fact is that we do not have enough of the tradition outside of Homer's poems to judge, on our own, pragmatically, Homer's relationship to his tradition. We know next to nothing, therefore, about the quality of other ancient Greek songs, although we know that such songs existed. We do not know whether they used formulas and themes in the ways in which Homer is alleged to use them. We do not know whether Homer was unique in this or whether this was a characteristic of his tradition.

Moreover, although we have materials for the study of the Serbo-Croatian songs, the actual study of them from this point of view has not been made. The publication of Medjedović's " The Wedding of Smailagić Meho " and of other songs as well, will give us even more and better texts and will enable us to make such a study. This is the task of those who know the languages involved. There is clearly much to be done. But until it is done it is premature to condemn the South Slavic poets out of hand. They deserve a more sympathetic hearing. While we can tell much about basic compositional techniques from the published songs—and there is still much for us yet to learn from them in this regard—we can also see in them, if we will, the seeds of expansion and variation of themes and of the possibility of the adjustment of themes to song context, to mention only two phenomena that have a bearing on Homeric practice.

I have already in *The Singer of Tales* pointed out briefly the intricate balances by various types of parataxis in line and passage construction in Salih Ugljanin's singing. We have noted also a similar tendency in themes to chiastic arrangements, as when a series of questions is answered in reverse order, a simple form of ring composition. Singers whose minds work in this orderly way cannot be said to be devoid of any aesthetic sense. Their poetics must be more fully studied before judgement is passed on the quality of their poems.

## OLD FRENCH

Ramon Menendez-Pidal's work (French translation 1960) in the field of Romance epic stands as the fullest review of Roland scholarship to its time and itself presents a statement of a form of traditionalism. It includes discussion of Jean Rychner's *La Chanson de Geste* (Geneva, 1955), a seminal work, which it takes to task for considering the *Roland* as atypical. For a bibliography of the problems of oral literature in the *chansons de geste* Menendez-Pidal's book, plus Joseph J. Duggan's *The Song of Roland: Formu-*

*laic Style and Poetic Craft* (Berkeley, 1973) and C. W. Aspland's *A Syntactical Study of Epic Formulas and Formulaic Expressions Containing the -ant Forms in Twelfth Century French Verse* (Queensland, 1970) are most helpful. Rychner's fine study of the style of the *chansons de geste* was marred only by the fact that he could not bring himself to include the *Roland* among those he was sure were oral traditional songs. It is from this point that Duggan takes his departure.

Duggan's published work in the field of formula study is the most valuable contribution so far in all three of the fields being considered here. Duggan has demonstrated in his analyses of formulas in the *chansons de geste* that density study is still very worth-while. By means of it he has been able to mark off distinct groups of poems, to differentiate the earlier *chansons* from the romances. I see no reason why this distinction, in the case of the *chansons de geste*, should not be understood as a distinction between oral and written.

Duggan's book contains an excellent general discussion of formula and theme, reviewing and commenting on the work of E. Villela de Chasca, R. Hitze, and others. But it goes far beyond the formula in its treatment of *Roland*. In illustrating why the *Roland* is greater than the other *chansons de geste*, Duggan has taken several planctus of the *Roland*, compared them with the planctus in other *chansons de geste*, and thus shown the superiority of the former. In this way he has demonstrated that one judges a traditional poet by comparison with other poets in the same tradition. Such a method, of course, depends on having enough of the tradition itself to use as a control of the themes involved. In this, Old French with its many texts is in a far better situation than any other medieval field. Duggan has also pointed out that in the *Roland* the similar laisses of the dramatic moments of the song are not found, for example, in the Baligant episode and in later *chansons*. This technique for similar laisses used to underscore heightened drama seems to have been developed in the *Roland* and appears to be a characteristic of an earlier period of the *chansons de geste*, a characteristic which was lost in time. These examples are of judgments of quality made in terms of oral traditional song itself, made from the point of view of the tradition, from the inside out, within the parameters traditional composition. Duggan's book is a model of this type of scholarship.

One of the most valuable recent doctoral dissertations in Old French epic studies is that of Tod N. Luethans, " Gormont et Isembart: A Description of the Epic as Seen in Light of the Oral Theory " (Harvard, 1972). Luethan's analysis of the battle themes in this rare octosyllabic Old French epic, together with its formulaic content, is a significant contribution to the study of oral literature.

## OLD ENGLISH

In 1953 Francis Peabody Magoun Jr.'s well-known article on *Beowulf* was published in *Speculum*, 28 (1953), 446-467, " The Oral Formulaic Character of Anglo-Saxon Narrative Poetry ". Its impact was felt widely in Anglo-

Saxon studies and to some extent elsewhere as well. A number of important doctoral dissertations were written under its influence. It was challenged in an article by Professor Larry D. Benson, "The Literary Character of Anglo-Saxon Formulaic Poetry", *PMLA* 81 (1966), 334-341, in which he demonstrated that there were many formulas in Anglo-Saxon poems that could not be oral traditional compositions but must be literary, even learned works, and thus he maintained that analyses of formulaic density are not necessarily a proof of oral composition. While formulas are characteristic, he stated, of oral poetry, and probably derived from it, they existed also in Anglo-Saxon literary poetry.

In her book *The Lyre and the Harp*, Ann Chalmers Watts in 1969 surveyed the situation of the oral-formulaic theory in respect to its application to Old English Poetry. In her conclusion she says:

"Unsatisfactory as it is, there seems to be no better evidence for the oral composition of ancient poetry than a high degree of formular phraseology. The degree must vary from language to language, verse-form to verse-form, and must be determined in each case ; but even though the untold loss of early poetical manuscripts must make the criterion of exactly repeated phraseology a rough gauge at best, still no other criterion comes as near to identifying for us the difference between phrases selected for their metrical efficacy and phrases not so selected. The rough gauge is hardly good enough to be useful. . . .

"The formulaic analysis of Old English texts may characterize what is on the page, but not the means by which it got there. This distinction is of paramount importance to the study of any "old" poetry less formulaic than Homer—that is, all un-Homeric poetry. . . . According to the arguments set forth at length in this book, the degree of formular phraseology in *Beowulf* and *Elene* is small by Homeric standards. At what point does a small degree of formular content become conventional diction in a literary composition as opposed to formular phraseology in an oral composition?"

In the opening of Professor Donald K. Fry's article, "Themes and Type-Scenes in *Elene*, 1-113", *Speculum*, XLIV, No. 1 (January, 1969), 35-45, the author makes the following assertion about the present state of formulaic studies in Anglo-Saxon:

"Formulaic studies of Old English poetry have come a long way since Francis P. Magoun's "Oral-Formulaic Character of Anglo-Saxon Narrative Poetry," published in 1953. Both opponents and proponents of the theory have found themselves moving closer together as the former survey the overwhelming body of evidence accumulating for formularity, and the latter begin to have serious doubts about the term "oral". Larry Benson's recent article, "The Literary Character of Anglo-Saxon Formulaic Poetry," marks a nexus of the two viewpoints, acknowledging both the definitely formulaic character of the verse and the lack of evidence for oral composition. The current stance could perhaps be summarized as hypothesizing a survival of formulaic technique in written poetry from an earlier oral tradition. At any rate, proof of oral composition would make little difference in assessing artistic success."

It appears from these two quotations that the effect of Benson's article was to free formula study from oral composition or, rather, to emphasize the formula as being derived from oral composition, but surviving to some degree into such work as the religious poems in Anglo-Saxon. The relationship of the style of such poems to the style of oral traditional poems or songs is a legitimate and worthwhile subject for investigation, as, indeed, is the study of the aesthetics of such poems, be they traditional or not.

There is, of course, in Anglo-Saxon only a small number of poems which from their subject matter could be traditional, even oral traditional. The most outstanding of these is, needless to say, *Beowulf*. We may have to leave it in limbo so far as the question of whether it is an oral traditional poem or not, because there simply is not enough possibly oral traditional material surviving in Anglo-Saxon for analysis. I might add that I must disagree with Fry on the final statement of the quotation above. I do believe that it is important " for assessing artistic success " to know whether a given text is part of an oral tradition or not. Otherwise the question of orality is not vital.

The basic concept of formulaic style is not complex, although its application in any given tradition or text or group of texts may present problems. For the sake of what follows, I should like to take a minute to recapitulate very briefly a view of oral composition. Language (at least, the Indo-European languages) especially spoken language (but also written language to the extent it follows the spoken language) is organized in substitution systems in repeated syntactic patterns. The formal language of law or religion has its set phrases and the lawyer or priest thinks and speaks under the proper circumstances in those set phrases. In fact, every group of specialists has its own characteristic repeated phrases, so that when one of its members speaks or writes he uses the phrases of his speciality. The same is true for the story teller in a traditional society, modern, medieval, or ancient, rural or urban. The matter of his stories is repetitive, and when an idea is repeated it most frequently is repeated in the same or very similar words. When a story is sung in verse, the requirements of the medium limit the possible choices of phrases more than does prose, and the repeated phrases become more noticeable, more " visible ". The formulas and the network of phrases like them are more numerous in traditional sung verse than in prose. They can be readily measured, particularly, as Duggan has well demonstrated, when computers are used.

From the narrowest point of view of text each performance is a new song, because the story is being told again without memorization of a non-existent fixed text, oral or written. The poet thus reconstructs his text each time, even as the story teller retells his story without concern for whether he uses the same words or not. The parallel is a useful one. On the other hand, the poet does not " improvise," that is to say, he does not make up consciously entirely new lines or entirely new passages. Just as a story teller, when he retells a story, will sometimes use the same sentences, or sentences very like the ones he has used before, so the singer in his story telling in verse will use lines he has used before, or lines like them. Neither of them consciously concerns himself or is even aware of whether he is using the same or slightly different or quite different phrases. Both of them are telling stories and are concentrating on that. What I am describing is that special kind of composition in verse that does not seek newness or originality, that is not afraid of using the old expressions—a special kind of " improvisation ", if you will, but not improvising out of whole cloth. In my attempts in the past to combat the idea of a fixed text that was memorized, I have apparently given the impression that not only is the text different at each singing by a given singer (which is true, of course), but that it is *radically* different, entirely improvised. This is not true. South Slavic oral epic is not, nor, to the best of my knowledge, is any oral traditional epic, the result of " free improvisation."

Because, however, of the restrictions of the verse, there emerges a number of more or less fixed phrases, lines, or groups of lines, i.e., the formulas and formulaic expressions of the poetry. *Both* these elements (formulas and formulaic expressions) are characteristic of this style. It has already been noted by others who were seeking to define the formula that the complex substitution systems that appear in an in-depth formulaic analysis are really equally, if not more, significant than the exactly repeated formulas. I suspect that a writer trying to imitate the oral traditional style would fix first on the repeated phrases, since they, as I have said, are more " visible." The true weaving of the style is more difficult, perhaps impossible, to imitate. Such a weave, with its formulas and formulaic expressions, might be considered to be the actual " oral " part of the style, since it is the necessity of rapid telling in the confines of song that has produced it.

There is, however, another part, the " traditional ", which has been little written about as such. This part is related directly to the subject matter of the songs, the ideas expressed by the story teller in song. That is to say, there is a specific given body of formulas and formulaic expressions, not just any phrases, but traditional phrases tied to the traditional ideas and subjects of the songs. Indeed, a tradition can be defined as the body of formulas, themes, and songs that have existed in the repertories of singers or story tellers in a given area over usually a long period of time.

Thus " oral " describes the weave of the style, and " traditional " defines the subject matter, the specific words and word combinations which express the ideas and set the specific patterns of the weave. It is, I believe, correct to speak of an " oral traditional " narrative song, using *both* terms. One should certainly not eliminate " oral " from this combination.

But do we find formulas outside of oral traditional sung verse? This question is the true thrust of Benson's article. It is clearly an important question, if we are to be able to use formulaic analysis for determining whether a text belongs to oral tradition or not, if the " rough gauge ", as Mrs Watts says, is to be " good enough to be useful ".

The first answer would be that one cannot have *formulas* outside of oral traditional verse, because it is the function of formulas to make composition easier under the necessities of rapid composition in performance, and if that necessity no longer exists, one no longer has formulas. If one discovers repeated phrases in texts known not to be oral traditional texts, then they should be called repeated phrases rather than formulas. I do not believe that this is quibbling about terms, because the distinction is functional. When one has said that, however, while one has clarified the terminology, one has not clarified the situation in the texts nor answered the question.

The fact of the matter is that the oral traditional style is easy to imitate by those who have heard much of it. Or, to put it another way, a person who has been brought up in an area, or lived long in one, in which he has listened to the singing and found an interest in it, can write verse using the general style and some of the formulas of the tradition. After all, the style was devised for rapid composition. If one wishes to compose rapidly in writing and comes from or has had much contact with an oral traditional poetry one not only can write in formulas, or something very like them, but normally does so. The style is natural to him. When the ideas are traditional the formulas may be those of the oral traditional poetry ; when the ideas are not traditional, they will not.

One should not overlook the possibility that such written poetry may set up formulas of its own for those ideas that do not come from the oral traditional poetry. The situation is extremely complicated, because one must keep in mind (a) that within the oral tradition itself, that is, within the group of practicing singers in the tradition, new ideas enter the songs, and (b) the poems written in the style of the tradition sometimes may influence the tradition itself. The question is whether one can tell by formulaic analysis the differences between the various kinds of poems. It seems clear that in order to be able to do this one must consider not only repetitions as such but the specific formulas used, or ideas expressed by them.

It is evident, therefore, that much more research will have to be done on texts of all kinds before any responsible answer to Benson's article can be given. In Anglo-Saxon research needs to be done not merely in numbers of formulas—although we could use still more definite statistics in this area —but also, and more particularly in specific formulas. That is to say, it would be useful to know, for instance, what formulas are common to *Beowulf* and to the religious poems, with attention paid, of course, to the Cynewulf poems as a unit and to the seemingly special relationship of *Andreas* to *Beowulf*. It would be helpful to know what formulas occur only in the religious poems—and so forth. The purpose is to determine not only whether a tradition exists but what its content is. We should also hope to find out more about the " weave " in Anglo-Saxon poetry. We already know a great deal about Anglo-Saxon poetry in these regards and compiling the rest of the information should not be too difficult. The same kind of investigation should be undertaken in other medieval poetries as well, such as Old French, Byzantine, and Old Spanish, insofar as materials are available.

It is ironical that we know considerably more about formulas in the Homeric poems and in Anglo-Saxon poetry than we do about them in a living narrative tradition. We urgently need further research in the Serbo-Croatian poetry and/or in that of other living narrative traditions. I have long been acutely aware that to date my formulaic analysis of a few of Salih Ugljanin's verses in *The Singer of Tales* is the main one on which we base our knowledge of oral traditional formulas in Serbo-Croatian. Kenneth Goldman's computer studies of formulas and formulaic systems in the songs of a Hercegovinian singer collected by Parry will be very valuable, and it is to be hoped that other investigations of pure traditional narrative poetry will be undertaken.

But the Serbo-Croatian material is especially pertinent to the study of both pure traditional songs and of all the various types and mixtures of written poetry as well. We have concentrated on the purity of the oral tradition, because one cannot investigate the mixed forms until the unadulterated form is well understood. In Serbo-Croatian literary history there is a unique situation, as far as I know, in which collecting of the traditional songs, and interest in them in general, led to writing what was thought to be that kind of poem. No less unique is the fact that both the tradition and the various mixtures can be documented by collected and published written texts over a period of more than two hundred years. R. Spraycar's paper, "The Oral-formulaic Character of Serbo-Croatian Poetry: A Reassessment", read before the Old English section of the MLA convention in Chicago, December 27, 1973, contains formulaic analysis of some lines of the eighteenth century Franciscan Andrija Kačić Mošić, who wrote a history of the South Slavs in prose and verse. His poetry is in the style of the traditional poems. We need many more analyses of such poems, including more of Kačić, as well as unpublished mixed texts in the Parry Collection. In the analyses attention should be given not only to the repetitions themselves, but even more importantly, to the weave of the style and to the specific formulas. What we seek is as full a description as possible of all facets of the style of an oral traditional narrative poetry and of its imitations and derivatives.

Benson's article has raised legitimate and vital questions which must be pursued fully until the whole truth of the several varieties of style involved and of their relationship to one another is clearly understood. It is certain that at the moment our knowledge of the facts is incomplete. We are fortunate that the material needed for such research is available in abundance.

Professor Fry's definitions of type-scene and theme are helpful in pointing up some of the difficulties in thematic study of oral traditional poetry. Here are his definitions as summarized in his 1969 article already mentioned above. They originally appeared in an earlier article, " Old English Oral-Formulaic Themes and Type-Scenes ", *Neophilologus* LII (1968), 48-54 :

"Most studies of Anglo-Saxon formulaic poetry have focused on the level of diction, that is, on the formulas themselves with some attention to systems of formulas. In Homeric and Yugoslavian scholarship, however, the emphasis has been on the next level of formulaic structure, the composition of the plot in stereotyped units, variously called 'motifs', 'type-scenes', 'action patterns', or 'themes.' . . . .

The definitions are as follows: A type-scene is a recurring stereo-typed presentation of conventional details used to describe a certain narrative event, requiring neither verbatim repetition nor a specific formula content ; and a theme is a recurring concatenation of details and ideas, not restricted to a specific event, verbatim repetition, or certain formulas, which forms an underlying structure for an action or description. Some typical type-scenes are sea-voyages, councils, and the arrival of a messenger. A series of such scenes connected by linking passages appropriate to the plot makes up a narrative ; the poet might, for example, compose a series such as banquet, damnation, approach to a city, exhortation, approach to battle, and battle itself (the poem so composed, of course, is *Judith*). The poet can repeat the same type-scene in one poem as many times as necessary, such as sea-voyages and banquets in *Beowulf*; and he can insert one type-scene into another, such as a council held during a banquet. A theme, on the other hand, is not tied to a specific narrative situation ; it provides a framework of imagery underlying the surface of narrative. So far only two themes have been isolated for study: the 'Hero on the Beach ' . . . and ' Exile.' "

Before discussing this passage from Fry, I should like to quote a condensed version of my comments on theme contained in a paper entitled, " The Marks of an Oral Style and their Significance ", read at meetings of the International Comparative Literature Association in Belgrade in 1967:

" Where shall we look on the story level for *narrative* criteria by which we can test whether any given text is from oral tradition or from literary tradition. Surely the theme is the answer. If, however, by theme one means *subject*, a narrative element, such as a catalogue, or a message, or equipping, or gathering of an army, then our definition is inadequate ; for clearly we can find gatherings of armies, equippings, messages, and catalogues in written as well as in oral literature. The theme as *subject* alone is too general for our very special purposes. But if by theme one means a repeated narrative element together with its verbal expression, that portion of a poem, an aggregate of specific verses, that tells a certain repeated part of the narrative, measureable in terms of lines and even words and word combinations, then we find ourselves dealing with elements of truly oral traditional narrative style. . . . Only thus is theme parallel on a "higher" level with formula. . . ."

" Themes are useful as aid in composition because they can be employed in more than one place in a song or in more than one song, and because the singer has a ready-made form for them, just as he has ready-made forms for formulas. He adjusts the formulas, to some extent, to a particular passage ; he also adjusts the themes, to some extent, to its particular environment in the song. No literary composer would tolerate the repeated use of the same passage, even if there were some slight verbal changes in it. When we find a passage used over and over again, we know it to be a theme, in the very technical sense applicable only to oral literature."

" Moreover, just as on the formula level in an oral poem almost everything is formula, so on the thematic level almost everything in a poem is theme. When one can analyze a kind of thematic density similar to the formulaic density of which we spoke earlier, this is another indication that the style of the poem involved is oral."

Although the repeated passages will not be word for word alike, there will be at least a sufficient degree of similarity of wording to show that the singer is using a unit of story that he holds already more or less formed in his mind. The closeness of text can be seen in the beginnings of three tellings of the same song by Salih Ugljanin. The song is " The Captivity of Dulić Ibrahim ", and the three texts are published in *Serbocroatian Heroic Songs*, Volume II, Nos. 4, 5 and 6, (see chart on p. 22).

There are some texts, of course, that show less verbal correspondence between occurrences of a theme, but the above demonstrates the kind of similarity in wording which is characteristic of what might be called a compositional theme. The chart also affords me the opportunity to remark that the kind of composition reflected in the three passages in it could not be described as " free improvisation." On the other hand, they could not be described as memorized passages either, nor as the product of a writer seeking originality of expression.

To return to a discussion of the quotation from Fry given above, it seems to me that his definition of theme is somewhat unclear and I shall concentrate on his comments on type-scene. It is noticeable in Anglo-Saxon and evident from Fry's treatment of type-scenes that there seems to be no, or at best very little, verbal correspondence between instances of type-scenes, and, therefore, it appears appropriate to differentiate them from the compositional themes with a reasonably high degree of verbal correspondence. The term " type-scene " performs this function very well.

Such type-scenes contain a given set of repeated elements or details, not all of which are always present, nor always in the same order, but enough of which are present to make the scene a recognizable one. David E. Bynum's doctoral dissertation in 1964 isolated the type-scenes (using the term "theme") in the songs about weddings in Serbo-Croatian oral epic. For each theme he listed the elements which were found in it. He examined some seventy-five songs and ascertained that all parts of the songs were themes, i.e., were repeated elsewhere in the tradition (or at least in the body of seventy-five

## No. 4

Ej! Đe sedimo, aj! da se veseljimo,
A da bi nas i Bog veseljijo,
Veseljijo, pa razgovorijo,
A lepšu ni sreću dijelijo
Na ovome mestu i svakome!
E! Sad veljimo da pesmu brojimo.
Davno nekad u zemanu bilo,
Davno bilo, sada pominjemo.

Jednom vaktu beše josvanulo,
E! U Zadaru pucaju topovi,
Dva zajedno ja trides' ujedno.
Stoji zemlje crne tutljavina.
Sve se svijet po čudi čudahu.
Šenlik čini jod Zadara bane.
Jufatijo slugu Radojicu,
E! Radojicu, tursku pridvoricu,
Pa ga tavnu bacilji zindanu.
Pa kad Rako ju tavnicu dođr,
E! Tu nađe trideset Turaka,
I među nji' Đuljić bajraktara,
A do njega Velagić Seljima.

Pa kad Rako ju tamnici dođe,
Dođe, stade, te him pomoj dade.
Sve mu age ljepše prifatiše,
Sve mu redom dobrodošle daje.

## No. 5

O starome vaktu i zemanu
Jedno jutro teke osamnulo,
Dva zajedno, trideset ujedno.

Ufatijo slugu Radojicu,
Radojicu, tursku pridvoricu,
Pa ga baci ljedenu zindanu.

Pa kad Rako u zindanu dođe,
Tuna nađe trideset Turaka,
I među nji' Đuljić Ibrahima,
I kraj njega Velagić Seljima,
I njihovo trides' i dva druga.

Pa him Rako pomoj naturijo,
A Turci mu bolje prifatilji.

## No. 6

Jednom vaktu a starom zemanu
Jedno jutro beše osvanulo,
U Zadaru pucaju topovi,

Sve se zemlja i planina trese.

Šenluk čini od Zadara bane.
Ufatio uskok Radovana,
Radojicu, tursku pridvoricu,
Pa ga baci ljedenu zindanu.

Pa kad Rako u tamnicu dođe,
Tuna nađe trideset Turaka,
A među nji' Đuljić Ibrahima,
I kod njega Velagić Selima.

Dođe Rako, pa him pomoj dade,
I svi njemu bolje prifatiše,
Pa mu redom dobrodošle daju.

songs which he investigated). Fry's method of identifying and describing type-scenes is generally the same as that used by Bynum in studying themes in Serbo-Croatian oral epic, and the results are similar. In both cases one finds a core of elements repeated within a frame. This kind of type-scene is characteristic of oral epic.

What distinguishes the type-scene from the theme (as I use the term) is the degree of verbal correspondence that makes the theme as such a distinctive feature of the oral compositional habit of a given singer. It (the theme) may also, although this has not been investigated, show regional differences, i.e., the habits of singers who listen to one another and belong to the same singing district.

In his analysis of type-scenes in *Elene* Fry has gone one step further, as have some Homerists as well, than defining and delimiting specific scenes. He has pointed out the way in which the poet shows his skill in composition and sensitivity by his handling of type-scenes. I find his analyses on the whole very convincing. He has, in short, moved into an aesthetics of thematic composition, a kind of composition that he is willing to call " traditional ", but which he hesitates to call oral, probably because of the strictures in Benson's article.

I would like to present the following suggestion for consideration. The men who knew the religious and saints' legends seem also at some time to have known an oral traditional poetry and its style, to have known it well enough to compose in it or in something similar to it. On the verse level the style may be marginal, not quite as formulaic in its repeated hemistichs as one might expect an oral traditional style to be, yet containing many hemistichs known from the oral traditional poetry such as that surrounding or behind *Beowulf*, if not *Beowulf* itself. This would account for the repeated phrases in poems like *Elene*, *Andreas*, and others. Although the composers of these poems might have known the saints' legends from sermons, i.e., not necessarily in written form, yet it is normal to assume that they knew them from some written source, for example, the Latin versions that were to be found in the monasteries. I would also like to suggest the possibility that in these poems, namely, the religious ones, a new body of formulas to express the new ideas of the Christian poetry was beginning to be developed on the model of the oral traditional poetry. I am tempted to call the religious poetry " transitional " or perhaps " mixed ". If that is the correct term, it applies not only to the formulas but to the themes as well.

If the religious poems were truly oral traditional songs, I would expect to find a higher degree of verbal correspondence among the various instances of a theme within a given poem, after making due allowance for adjustment to the specific position in the poem which it occupies. It may possibly be that the necessity that gave rise to themes with close verbal correspondence no longer existed or was felt. But the theme with its elements persists and is operative as a model for composition and as a base for multiforms. As

Fry has demonstrated, in this respect the theme was still a living force in composition, and the audience for the poems must have been still enough of a traditional audience to feel that the working out of these models was right.

In sum, the increase in the last few years in the number of studies of oral literature is very encouraging. We are learning about many aspects of this phenomenon in many hitherto either unexplored or inadequately described traditions. Our analyses of medieval and ancient texts have somewhat outdistanced our knowledge of the processes of living traditions. But work in progress is slowly lessening that gap. There is emerging a degree of moderation in aesthetic studies of medieval and ancient texts in consideration of traditional and/or oral characteristics found in them. In this regard our greatest need is for further investigation of the aesthetics of oral traditional narrative poetries. Finally, although I have spoken almost exclusively of stylistic matters, because it is through style that we have tried to identify and characterize oral literature, one should not forget the many other aspects of oral literature, above all its function and its meaning.

ALBERT B. LORD

*Harvard*

# PARALLEL VERSIONS OF
# "THE BOYHOOD DEEDS OF CUCHULAINN"

The *Cattle Raid of Cooley* (*Táin Bó Cúailnge*) is the longest and most important surviving medieval Irish saga. The two major surviving texts of the saga are those of *Lebor na hUidre*[1] ("the *Book of the Dun Cow* "), largely written down by a scribe who was killed in 1106,[2] and of the so-called *Book of Leinster*,[3] compiled in the second half of the twelfth century.[4] The language of the earliest version can be dated to the ninth century, and some poetic passages may be even older. Although several types of poetry appear in the sagas, the bulk of the narrative is in prose.

Because of the difficulty of the language and the inaccessibility of the texts, scholarly work on early Irish saga did not really begin until the latter part of the last century, and, as a result, many questions, long ago answered for other literatures, remain to be solved in regard to the Irish sagas. Problems of narrative structure are especially vexing, for we know little about the authorship, intentionality, or audience of these sagas. We do know that they were written down by clerics, and, on the other hand, that Ireland had a long tradition of professional oral transmission of literature and lore of all kinds.[5] But the relationship between the oral literary traditions and the written texts as we have them is far from clear.

Some attention has been paid lately to the possibilities of using the techniques of formulaic analysis on medieval Irish material, but what little work has so far appeared along these lines has been of a highly tentative nature.[6] My aim here is to demonstrate, using comparative methods, that at least one section of the *Cattle Raid of Cooley*, the "Boyhood Deeds of Cúchulainn" (*macgnímrada*), provides strong evidence for a long oral

---

[1] Ed. R. I. Best and Osborn Bergin (Dublin: Royal Irish Academy, 1929), pp. 142-206 ; hereafter referred to as " LU ". For an excellent recent English trans. see Th. Kinsella, *The Táin* (London: Oxford U.P., 1970). I use the word " medieval " throughout in a non-specific way to cover the seventh to fourteenth centuries, not to classify formally the language of the texts under discussion, which are written in Old and Middle Irish.

[2] See LU, p. xii and J. V. Kelleher, " The *Táin* and the Annals ", *Ériu*, XXII (1971), 107-27.

[3] Cecile O'Rahilly, ed. and trans., *Táin Bó Cúalnge from the Book of Leinster* (Dublin: Inst. for Advanced Stud., 1967) ; hereafter, " LL ".

[4] W. O'Sullivan, " Notes on the Scripts and Make-up of the Book of Leinster ", *Celtica*, VII, (1966), 1-31.

[5] For the most widely accepted modern views on the subject of oral transmission in Ireland see: David Greene, " Early Irish Literature ", in *Early Irish Society*, ed. Myles Dillon (Dublin: Cultural Relations Comm. of Ireland, 1954), pp. 22-35, and Gerard Murphy, *Saga and Myth in Ancient Ireland* (Dublin: Cultural Relations Comm. of Ireland, 1954).

[6] For example, Kevin O'Nolan, " Homer and the Irish Hero Tale ", *Studia Hibernica*, VIII, (1968), 7-20 ; James Ross, " Formulaic Composition in Gaelic Oral Literature ", *Mod. Philol.*, LVII, No. 1 (1959), 1-12 ; and Cecile O'Rahilly, op. cit., p. xlviii, n. 1. For the most recent work on the subject see Edgar M. Slotkin, " Evidence for Oral Composition in Early Irish Saga ", Diss. Harvard 1973.

history for at least part of this important saga, and also helps to demonstrate that the formal narrative structure of the " Ulster Cycle " tales, of which the *Cattle Raid of Cooley* is the centrepiece, as we find them in manuscript, owes much to the traditions and methods of oral composition. It may be impossible ever to make a final determination of " orality " for a given text, but at least we can work toward a surer sense of compositional standards and audience in medieval Ireland.

It is noticeable to almost any reader of the *Cattle Raid of Cooley* in the original (or even in a good translation)—especially in the *Book of the Dun Cow* version—that there is something stylistically odd about the " Boyhood Deeds " section. It is compact, self-contained, interrupts the flow of the narrative about the advance of the host, is told as a flashback, contains no *roscada*,[7] and adds nothing to the story of the cattle raid itself except some background on Cúchulainn's early life. Many scholars, notably James Carney and Frank O'Connor,[8] have argued that the " Boyhood Deeds " section represents an interpolation of later material into a more archaic text of the saga, but there are powerful reasons for seeking an alternative explanation for the change in style. The *Cattle Raid of Cooley* has survived in no less than ten manuscripts and manuscript-fragments, no one of which seems to have been copied directly from any other, and among which there are at least three (and perhaps four or more) " recensions ".[9] With so many variants in existence, the entire question of what constitutes an " interpolation " (which pre-supposes a fixed text into which something can be interpolated) seems to me to be problematic in the extreme.

To complicate the matter even further, the versions of the " Boyhood Deeds " presented in the *Book of the Dun Cow* and *Book of Leinster*, while sharing the same basic set of incidents for the most part, differ in one very important respect. The *Book of the Dun Cow* version contains five incidents which do not appear in the *Book of Leinster*, and scholars have been at something of a loss to explain just what they are doing there.[10] In her excellent introduction to the *Book of Leinster* text of the *Cattle Raid of Cooley*, Cecile O'Rahilly discusses the problem as follows:

§§ 12-15.[11] All this extra material is an addition to Fergus's narration in the *Macgnímrada* section. Conall Cernach's account which follows

---

[7] *Rosc* or *roscad*: A type of syntactically and semantically obscure archaic (or archaized) verse, usually cadenced, sometimes designated by a marginal ".r." in Irish manuscripts. On the use of the term see, P. MacCana, " On the Use of the Term *Retoiric* ", *Celtica*, VII, (1966), 65-90.

[8] James Carney, *Studies in Irish Literature and History* (Dublin, 1955), p. 67 ; Frank O'Connor, *Leinster, Munster and Connaught* (London, 1950), pp. 154-55.

[9] For my objections to the use of Lachmannian manuscript filiation techniques on medieval Irish prose narrative, see my unpublished doctoral diss., " Narrative Structure in Irish Saga ", Harvard 1972.

[10] See Appendix A. I will henceforth refer to these five " extra " incidents as " Version B " and the rest of the incidents as " Version A ".

[11] Version B. The numbers here refer to textual divisions in R. Thurneysen's *Die Irische Helden- und Königsaga* (Halle: Niemeyer, 1921).

is of one exploit only, the killing of Culann's hound. So too, in the last section, Fiacha describes how the boy takes up arms and first wields them. But in Recension I, Fergus describes not one but several exploits. The words *Fecht n-and dano, or Fergus, in tan ba gilla* [" ' There was a time ', said Fergus, ' when he was a lad ', "] . . . introducing this extra material are superfluous here and suggest the addition of a compiler. There is repetition too in the account of Cú Chulainn's ball-playing with the youths in *Aided na Macraide* [" The Death of the Boytroop "]. In Fergus's opening story § 11 Cú Chulainn merely knocks down the boys in Emain. In Conall's account § 16 he kills a hound. But Fiacha's story § 17 reaches a climax when the boy kills three of the Ulstermen's enemies and bears their bloody heads in triumph to Emain, while a childish touch is added by representing him as carrying in equal triumph the birds and deer that he has captured alive. With the extra matter §§ 12-15 there is no sense of climax, for in that part Cú Chulainn is said to have killed again and again. It has sometimes been suggested that the whole of the *Macgnímrada* section, containing neither verse nor rhetorics, is an interpolation in TBC. Here, however, I suggest only that the extra material in Fergus's narration was added at some time by some compiler of Recension I who could not leave well alone. Without the passages §§ 12-15 the *Macgnímrada* section is more consistent and more artistically satisfying. This perhaps might be made an argument in favour of a skilful compiler of the LL-version who condensed to the advantage of the narrative. But I think that this is to attribute too great a power of constructive imagination to the LL-compiler.[12]

This view assumes that whoever added the additional episodes did so out of a simple lack of taste, and it is true that the extra stories of Version B do seem to lack the nice coherence of the ones shared by the two texts of Version A. But there are reasons beyond *our* sense of aesthetics why a medieval Irish scribe would add these particular episodes to an already full version of Cúchulainn's *macgnímrada*. In my view, the interpolator, whoever he might have been and whenever he might have been active, knew another version, " recension ", if you will, and felt that the story was incorrect as it stood ; thus we are dealing with a question more of pseudohistorical accuracy than of aesthetics. Thurneysen himself postulated two " original " versions of the *Cattle Raid of Cooley*[13] and, although his views on this question seem rather over-simplified today, it is true that we really can make no firm judgment as to whether Version B was interpolated into Version A, or Version A interpolated around Version B, since we have no way of recreating the history of the compilation of our earliest surviving manuscript of the story—a manuscript which already contains both versions. But the entire problem becomes less vexing if we view Versions A and B of the " Boyhood Deeds " as alternative parallel versions of exactly the same story, carrying in slightly different form exactly the same messages,

[12] Pp. xxxiv-v.
[13] Op. cit., p. 112.

but far enough apart to convince a later medieval Irish scribe that one version contained historical information which supplemented the other. See Appendix A for the outline and arrangement of the tales.

Several generalizations can be made from the arrangement of the incidents themselves. First, it is clear that the " Boyhood Deeds " as we have them were clearly regarded as some sort of unit by those who were writing them down. There is even a hint in the *Book of Leinster* that they may have circulated separately from the body of the *Cattle Raid of Cooley*: " Some say that the tales before the *Táin* should also include Cúchulainn's coming to the house of Culann the smith, Cúchulainn's taking up arms and mounting into his chariot, and Cúchulainn's journey to the boy-troop in Emain Macha. But these three tales are given in the body of the *Táin*."[14] Because of its episodic nature, the *Cattle Raid of Cooley* must have lent itself to various kinds of abstraction, and thus I would hesitate to draw very firm conclusions about the relationship of independent versions of the " Boyhood Deeds " to the tales as they appear in the *Cattle Raid* itself ; but whatever the origin of these tales, the problem of what they are doing where we find them remains. Aside from the negative evidence that we do not, in fact, find these tales scattered around various manuscripts outside the texts of the *Cattle Raid of Cooley* (as are, for instance, the death tales of many of the Ulster heroes), we know that Versions A and B of the " Boyhood Deeds " must have been combined prior to the compilation of the *Book of the Dun Cow*, for another manuscript, the *Yellow Book of Lecan*, contains a version of the *Cattle Raid of Cooley* clearly drawn from the same examplar. Additionally, the incidents of Version A are virtually identical in the *Book of Leinster* and *Book of the Dun Cow-Yellow Book of Lecan* versions of the *Cattle Raid*, indicating that the *Book of Leinster* compiler either excised Version B, or was unaware of it. The language of the *Book of Leinster* text, however, differs considerably from that of the *Book of the Dun Cow* text.

I would also argue that the *macgnímrada* were considered a part of the *Cattle Raid of Cooley* from the time that it was put together as an entity since, the comment cited above from the *Book of Leinster* aside, we have no version of the saga that lacks it.[15] Two discrete sets of tales about the boyhood deeds of the hero Cúchulainn are combined in an early text of the saga, but only one set appears in a later text.

Like all stories that are more than a bare outline, the " Boyhood Deeds " in the *Cattle Raid of Cooley* have a good deal of what I would call " aesthetic depth "—there is no single explanation or characterization which can convey everything conveyed by reading or hearing the stories in their entirety.

[14] Trans. by Kinsella, op. cit., p. 2 ; for text see, *The Book of Leinster*, ed. R. I. Best and M. A. O'Brien, V, (Dublin : Inst. for Adv. Stud., 1967), p. 1119, lines 32905-9.

[15] Including, by inference, the apparently widely variant version known to the *Book of the Dun Cow* interpolator, " H " (see Appendix A), who almost certainly would have changed it if he felt it necessary. He confined himself, however, to a few grammatical emendations in the text of the *macgnímrada*.

Many messages are being transmitted at once in such complex stories and I propose to try to take the *macgnímrada* apart, as one would the strands of a rope, in hopes of elucidating some of the basic, and sometimes concealed, meanings. This process will, to some extent, enable us to find out something about the original audience (of the time when the story was truly alive and not simply a piece of quaint lore) for the saga, in the form in which we have it.

On the most obvious level, the message that Cúchulainn is a precocious youth who has grown to be a hero, like Herakles or Sigurd, is inescapable ; and, superficially at least, one can say that for the purpose of the larger story his precocious heroism cannot simply be stated, but must be illustrated graphically. Cúchulainn must be *shown* to be a hero and the most fitting representative of the Ulstermen. There is a great deal more being conveyed, though, by these stories, and much of the information is implicit in the narrative structure of the tales themselves.

Taking first Version A, we note the curious fact that in psychological terms each incident is a microcosm of the entire series of stories. In its barest terms, the action is in each case:

1. Cúchulainn enters from outside.
2. He asserts himself against the men of Ulster.
3. He is accepted by the Ulstermen as a warrior (several times by King Conchobor himself.)

The pattern of the " Boyhood Deeds " as a whole, in Version A, is a larger scale exposition of the same psychological events:

1. Cúchulainn's arrival and introduction to the Ulstermen over opposition.
2. Cúchulainn's gaining of his name against opposition.
3. Cúchulainn's taking arms over the druid's objections.
4. Cúchulainn's joining the warriors over Conall's objections.
5. Cúchulainn's killing of three enemies against his charioteer's repeated warnings.
6. Cúchulainn's capturing wild food in spite of his charioteer's objections.
7. Cúchulainn's return to Emain in a dangerous frenzy and his reacceptance by the king.

In each case, Cúchulainn has entered a situation where he has no apparent right according to ordinary judgments of his appearance (of youth), and in each case he forces recognition of his new status as an included individual. In the *macgnímrada* as a whole, he does exactly the same thing. To put it most simply, even though he is only one-half Ulsterman by birth, and a mere child, he forces himself into the warrior class of Ulster and is accepted. The pattern of *arrival, opposition,* and final *acceptance* is emphasized by repetition in varying contexts. This sequence is a striking example of the fact that sheer repetition—often seen elsewhere in Irish saga as

" doubling ", to use Thurneysen's word—can carry significant meaning in itself in early literature, as Albert Lord has pointed out.[16] That such repetition is essentially a characteristic (because a necessity) of orally composed literature, does not disturb the argument in regard to an early written text, for the necessities of oral literature become the clichés of early written literature. It is also worth mentioning in passing, that in three of the episodes in the " Boyhood Deeds ", Cúchulainn's close connection with Conchobor, his mother's brother, is emphasized. The uncle-nephew relationship, especially in regard to a sister's son, shows up in so many works of early literature in the Indo-European world, and in other cultures with similar social structure, that its repetition and consequent emphasis here must be expressive of considerable original importance.

If there is an underlying psychological message contained in the order of incidents in Version A, which tells over and over again the story of Cúchulainn's initiation into warriorhood and his true relationship to the rest of the Ulstermen, what then does the addition of the incidents of Version B do to this nice, internally consistent, initiation tale ? By displaying an orderly sequence of events showing Cúchulainn forcing his way into Ulster warrior society and demonstrating in turn each of the attributes necessary for entry into that society, Version B conveys exactly the same sequence of messages that we find in Version A. In such a context, statements based on a modern aesthetic such as, " With the extra matter §§ 12-15 there is no sense of climax, for in that part Cú Chulainn is said to have killed again and again ",[17] lose meaning, for if Version B is a parallel version of the *macgnímrada*, then there is no reason why we should expect the growth of Cúchulainn's killing power, used as an index of his warriorhood with some subtlety in Version A, to be used in Version B as well.

In fact, it is clear that Version B deals with Cúchulainn's initiation into warriorhood in quite different terms than does Version A, but carries exactly the same message and thus is not an ornament, but in origin a functional substitute. We have here two independent versions of the same hero's initiation story combined by someone unaware of their equivalence. The structure of all incidents or moves in Version B is not completely identical with the overall pattern, but the message put forward about arrival, opposition, and acceptance seems to be the same.

1. Cúchulainn demands (by force) a special bed and the right to sleep undisturbed. His demands are met.[18]
2. Cúchulainn asserts his rights against the boytroop and is armed by Conchobor.

---

[16] *Singer of Tales* (New York: Atheneum, 1965), p. 220.

[17] O'Rahilly, p. xxxv.

[18] That this story may be onomastic, and also that it is an explanation for why Cúchulainn was not awake in a later incident, does not affect the fact that it is functionally an expression of arrival, opposition and acceptance in this particular cluster of incidents.

3. Cúchulainn saves Conchobor and obtains food (after ignoring a warning.)

4. Cúchulainn kills three groups of the enemies of Ulster by himself.

This sequence of events covers exactly the same ground covered by Version A. Cúchulainn comes to the Ulstermen from outside and asserts himself (by demanding sleep and an unusual bed), overcomes and separates himself from the boytroop, and is accepted by his uncle, Conchobor. He then saves Conchobor (who, as king, represents all Ulster), obtains food, and finally kills three units of Ulster's enemies. Except for the reversal of food-gathering and triple-slaying, this is the same sequence of events that we find in Version A. It is also worth mentioning that Cúchulainn is wounded in the last incident in Version B and thus incapacitated for doing any damage to his own people in his battle-fury.

If it is indeed the case that Version B is a parallel and equivalent version of the " Boyhood Deeds of Cúchulainn," though less elaborated than Version A, and included by some earlier compiler for reasons of pseudo-historical completeness, it would help to clarify what has been suggested of the *Book of Leinster* version's compiler: that he was working from a " stripped down " version of Recension I.[19] Perhaps he was using only one of a series of complete and parallel versions available to the compiler responsible for the *Book of the Dun Cow* text. It is significant that Version B seems to be a unit as well as Version A ; we do not find its stories split up and scattered around in medieval manuscripts.

Since Version A and Version B appear to be functional narrative equivalents, and since both, as I will show below, seem to be outgrowths of a common Indo-European narrative tradition, as well as being composed of discrete incidents which are themselves thematic equivalents of the initiation pattern as a whole, but since, on the other hand, Version A and Version B are not close enough in expression to have been derived, however remotely, from some common manuscript source, nor recognized as equivalents by whoever combined them, I think we are left with the almost inescapable conclusion that they are in origin independent multiform oral variants of a common story pattern, committed, by an as yet unknown process, to writing. And this conclusion, in turn, hints at a living tradition in Ireland perhaps as late as the eleventh century. The possibility that one or both of these variants originated in written rather than oral form cannot, of course, be completely ruled out, but the thematic patterning and great antiquity of subject matter make a written genesis for either version seem the less likely hypothesis.

The importance of the shape of the action to the meaning of this initiation story can be demonstrated most clearly by turning to comparable initiation stories in the saga and myth of other Indo-European cultures. Georges

[19] O'Rahilly, p. xlv.

Dumézil has argued in *Horace et les Curiaces*[20] that the stories of victory by a young hero against a triple adversary found in the " Boyhood Deeds of Cúchulainn," the story of Horace and the Curiatii as told by Livy, and several other Indo-European mythological histories, represent a narrative version of a ritual initiation of young warriors in early Indo-European societies which survived in literature long after the practice had died because of the symbolic value of the stories themselves in presenting the real concerns of the societies in regard to warmaking functions and fertility.[21]

Backed by numerous examples from Roman and Greek sources, Dumézil argues that the stories of Cúchulainn in the *macgnímrada* and of Horatius in Livy[22] display exactly the same pattern of action in spite of their apparent differences in style and form[23]. Briefly, the story of the three Horatii is as follows: to avert a mass slaughter of their troops, the Romans and their Etruscan enemies decide to settle an impending war by single (in this case, triple) combat. The Romans send forth the Horatian triplets and the Etruscans send the Curiatii. Livy specifically states that both sets of triplets were volunteers. The battle takes place in full view of both armies and, although his two brothers are killed almost immediately, Horatius manages to separate the Curiatii and kill them one by one. Flushed with triumph on behalf of his people, Horatius returns to the gates of Rome only to find his sister weeping because he has killed her fiancé who was one of the Curiatii. Enraged at her " shamelessness " in his hour of triumph, he stabs his sister to death. In spite of his victory, young Horace is immediately convicted of sororicide, but is not executed for his crime. Instead, he is made to perform certain unspecified purification rites which Livy says, " became from that day traditional in the Horatian family ",[24] and to walk under a yoke called the " sister's beam ".

In comparing Cúchulainn's initiation, as told in the " Boyhood Deeds " with Livy's story of the Horatii and Curiatii, Dumézil sees several essential points of identity: the victory of the young hero against a triple adversary, his return to the city of his people in a heroic fury, his encounter with a " shameless " relative of the opposite sex, his restraint by the authorities of the city (tribe) and his final re-integration into society by a purification rite[25] These parallels are certainly there and the chance of their being coincidentally identical seems remote, especially since the battle with the three-headed monster is known from other Indo-European mythic tradi-

[20] St Amand, 1942.

[21] Although Dumézil's tripartite division of Indo-European society does seem to apply rather better to ancient Ireland than to many other societies, it is not necessary to accept his views totally to sustain the argument I make here.

[22] Livius, (Titus) Patavinus, *The Early History of Rome*, Bks. I-IV, trans. A. de Sélincourt (Harmondsworth: Penguin, 1960).

[23] His later book, *Aspects de la fonction guerrière chez les Indo-Européens* (Paris, 1956), expands the comparison by including Indian myth.

[24] Op. cit., p. 47.

[25] *Horace*, p. 88.

tions ; for instance, the killing of a three-headed monster by the youngest of the Aptya triplets in the *Rig Veda*[26]—followed by a necessary ritual purification because the monster was a Brahman ; and (more problematically) Thorr's duel with Hrungnir, who had a three-cornered heart of stone.

In my view, the parallels between the " Boyhood Deeds' and the story of Horatius are more numerous than Dumézil has indicated. To his list I would add the fact that Cúchulainn's battle with the sons of Nechta is in spite of warnings from others, while the Horatii are warned by their commander before they volunteer, and the fact that Cúchulainn is accompanied by his charioteer who isn't much help, just as Horatius' brothers are no help. Dumézil does note that the encounter with Conall Cernach serves to emphasize Cúchulainn's peculiar state in this incident—accompanied, but alone.[27]

Dumézil purposely ignored Version B in his discussion, on the grounds that the incidents it contains were a trivial ornamentation, but in fact, they repay careful consideration. If Version A and Version B are indeed parallel versions of the same story, and if Dumézil is correct in his analysis of Version A as reflecting in some way an Indo-European initiation ritual, then Version B must contain the same elements—the same sequential cluster of ideas— as Version A. It does. In both cases the essential elements of initiation are present: the separation from the other young men, the defeat of the triple adversary in singlehanded defense of one's people, and the purification of the initiate. In regard to the element of purification clearly present in Version A and in the story of the Horatii, I have made the suggestion above that the fact that Cúchulainn sustains fifty wounds in the fight with the Fir Faichi indicates that the same idea—that of restraining the battle-fury of the hero—is being symbolized here. Another interesting point to be noted about Version B is the extreme emphasis given to threesomes by repetition. The men of the Isles of Faiche come in three groups of nine—not, to be sure, an unusual configuration in early Irish saga—but Cúchulainn kills nine, or one-third of them and, although the word used is *nonbor* (" a group of nine men "), I suspect we are to imagine his killing three from each group, rather than wiping out one group altogether, a motif which has a parallel in the tale *The Wooing of Emer*.[28]

But Dumézil goes a step farther than his postulation of an Indo-European initiation rite in his discussions of the stories of Cúchulainn's boyhood feats and the victory of Horatius over the Etruscan triplets. He ties the ideas behind the stories to the system of tripartite organization which he feels is peculiar to the Indo-Europeans and their mythology. Whether anyone be-

[26] See Dumézil, *Aspects,* passim.

[27] *Horace,* p. 105.

[28] *Tochmarc Emire,* for text see *Compert Con Culainn,* ed. A. G. Van Hamel, Med. and Mod. Irish Ser. III (Dublin: Inst. for Adv. Stud., 1956), p. 63. For trans. see T. P. Cross and C. H. Slover, eds., *Ancient Irish Tales* (N.Y., 1936), p. 170, or Kinsella, op. cit., p. 37.

sides the Indo-Europeans had such a system, it is fairly clear that the Indo-Europeans did, and that expression of it is extremely important in their symbolic remains. It is at this level that some of the underlying messages of the *macgnímrada* begin to come clear—real and important philosophical messages about warriors and adolescents. To understand the stories of the " Boyhood Deeds " on their own terms we must treat them, as we must treat all early literature, as communication systems.

In *Horace et les Curiaces* and in an expanded fashion in *Aspects de la fonction guerrière*, Dumézil argues that the initiation story typified by the victory of Horace and Cúchulainn's initiation as an Ulsterman is a graphic description of the very real social problems posed by a warrior caste in early Indo-European society. Each caste or " function " according to Dumézil has its own job to do in the total organism of society—sovereignty, war, or fertility—but it is a striking feature of the warrior class that the more successfully it is able to fulfil its function, the more dangerous it is to the society which it serves. The uncontrollable violence which characterizes the superb warrior—for instance, Cúchulainn's *riastrad* (" heroic distortion ")— is a clear danger to the warrior's own community if not checked by some means, for example, Cúchulainn's immersion, or Horace's performance of the " Horatian Rites " and passage under the yoke to symbolize his submission to the rest of the state. In completing his initiation, the young Indo-European warrior symbolized the necessary submission of his caste to the society as a whole: " Then he got out and Mugain the queen gave him a blue cloak to go around him with a silver brooch in it, and a hooded tunic. And he sat on Conchobor's knee, and that was his seat ever after."[29]

But what are the naked women doing in the story ? Dumézil's answer, again I think the correct one, is that the contrast between warlike and sexual energy is being stressed. The channeling of adolescent energy and interest at puberty is put in its most concrete contrastive terms—Cúchulainn is confronted with undisguised feminity and sexuality just at the point when his warlike fury is most dangerous, and is forced to hesitate long enough to be cooled down. Horatius is likewise confronted with his sister in a state emphasizing her sexuality—mourning her husband-to-be—and is made to undergo a rite of submission as a result of the encounter. All these ideas are expressed concretely enough through the arrangement of incidents in the stories, and it is recognition of these patterns of meaningful action that leads to the conclusion that Version B is an alternate telling of Version A of the " Boyhood Deeds ".

Thus we can see that this initiation story has meaning beyond what its surface appearance would suggest, and that the very close comparative Indo-European material shows its real antiquity of subject matter and plot, whatever it may have meant to later Irish pseudo-historians and scribes. This evidence for antiquity means that even if the " Boyhood Deeds "

[29] Kinsella, p. 92.

section was put together in the form we find it in and dropped bodily into the *Cattle Raid of Cooley* at a late date in the manuscript transmission, it still represents the kind of genuine early tradition we see in much of the rest of the saga, for it is clear that to take any of the *Cattle Raid* as some sort of historical record is misleading. Like any other work of epic or early literature, it takes place in a psycho-synthetic world of metaphor, and it is the metaphor embodied in the concrete structure of the story which gives such tales much of their original meaning. After all, there are few who would read the *Odyssey* simply as a travel book ; Odysseus' return to his kingdom and family is a figurative journey as well as a real one, and the route he takes at least partially predetermined by earlier story patterns.[30]

The point that the *Cattle Raid of Cooley* is neither completely original nor independent of earlier story patterns has been made elsewhere.[31] In a more particular sense, the same kind of evidence can be used to demonstrate that the " Boyhood Deeds " probably formed part of the saga from an early period. I do not mean to argue that the texts of the " Boyhood Deeds " as we have them are extremely old compositions, for the language in neither case seems to antedate the text by very much. In dealing with early literature, however, manuscript age is not always the surest test of the age of a story. As for the argument that the *macgnímrada* are a late compilation dropped into the saga, we do have one piece of evidence, aside from that of language and style, that it was not part of all versions of the saga (see above, p. 27). But, once again, I think it is the structure of the narrative that gives us a clue to what the place of the " Boyhood Deeds " in the *Cattle Raid of Cooley* is, for the plot of the saga is unique neither in Irish nor in Indo-European tradition. The *macgnímrada* fill a slot in the saga which is paralleled elsewhere.

Cúchulainn's life is essentially a recreation of the career of his father, the god Lug, and the " Boyhood Deeds " in the *Cattle Raid of Cooley* form an essential part of this pattern. On a superficial level, a case can be made for the idea that it is necessary that Cúchulainn's initiation be described, since he is about to be introduced as the adversary of the men of Ireland, and, because he is very young, the fact that he has received his initiation as a warrior is not trivial in this context. The initiation episode probably belongs here, however, for a far deeper reason. One of the central features of the *Cattle Raid of Cooley* is Cúchulainn's lone defense of Ulster. In this he follows the pattern set by his father, Lug, in the tale called the " Second Battle of Moytura " ;[32] the story of how Cúchulainn came to represent all

[30] The close parallels between, for instance, Circe in the *Odyssey* and Ishtar in the Mesopotamian *Gilgamesh Epic*, have often been noted. See *Singer of Tales*, Ch. viii.

[31] See, for example, my diss. (cited above) or Alwyn and Brinley Rees, *Celtic Heritage* (London: Thames and Hudson, 1961).

[32] For text, from Brit. Mus. MS. Harley 5280, see Wh. Stokes, *Rev. Celt.*, XII, and R. Thurneysen, *Zeitschr. f. Celt. Philol.* XII ; for text, from RIA MS. 24 P 9 (a later version), see Brian Ó Cuív, *Cath Muighe Tuireadh* (Dublin: Inst. for Adv. Stud., 1945). For trans. see Cross and Slover, pp. 28 ff.

the warriors of Ulster fills the same part of the pattern that Lug's taking the throne of the Tuatha Dé Danann[33] fills in the " Second Battle of Moytura."

The pattern of Lug's life as related in the " Second Battle of Moytura ":

1. He is only one-half Tuatha Dé Danann by birth.
2. He appears at the great hall of the Tuatha Dé and is not recognized.
3. He proves himself to the heroes of the Tuatha Dé and is recognized as *Samildanach* (roughly, " possessor of all arts ").
4. He stands in for Nuadu, king of the Tuatha Dé.
5. He defeats the enemies of the Tuatha Dé singlehanded.
6. He captures the god Bres and gains the secrets of fertility from him.

The pattern of Cúchulainn's life as told in the " Ulster Cycle " tales:

1. He is only one-half Ulsterman by birth. (*Compert Con Culainn*).
2. He appears at Emain Macha, the Ulster court, and is not recognized. (*Táin Bó Cúailnge*)
3. He proves himself to the warriors. (the *macgnímrada* in the *Táin*)
4. He stands in for all the Ulstermen. (*Táin*)
5. He defeats the enemies of Ulster singlehanded. (*Táin*)[34]
6. He ensures fertility by marrying suitably. (*Tochmarc Emire*)[35]

This patterning, I think, makes it clear what the " Boyhood Deeds " are doing in the *Cattle Raid of Cooley*, and in this position in the saga— before the first battle between Cúchulainn and the men of Ireland. The cataloging of Cúchulainn's feats of strength and agility in the tales of the *macgnímrada*, his gaining of a new name, his taking his place in the tribe although only an Ulsterman on his mother's side, and his victory in battle against the advice of his elders, all take place in the same order as the adventures of his father in the " Second Battle of Moytura ", and this exact paralleling of action would have given extra resonance to the tales in a milieu in which both narratives were known. Thus I think that the ordering of events in the *Cattle Raid of Cooley* can be shown to have a patterning of some antiquity in Ireland and that, whatever he did with his materials, or however well he understood them, the compiler of the " Boyhood Deeds " was dealing with material which had taken shape long before he came to use it. A similar pattern can be found in the great Indian epic, the *Māhābhārata*, which contains a section on the training and initiation of the heroes and of their half-brother Karna in the first book.

Thus in the *macgnímrada* in the *Táin Bó Cúailnge*, we see the continuing

[33] " Tribe of the Goddess Danu "—mythological invaders of Ireland.

[34] A further parallel here is that Lug kills the Fomorian giant Balor in the " Second Battle of Moytura ", while Cúchulainn kills the Fomorian, Forgall the Wily in " The Wooing of Emer ". The Fomorians were the mysterious and dangerous enemies of the Tuatha Dé Danann.

[35] In spite of the fact that the marriage is childless, I think it can be regarded as a reflex of a " sacred marriage " motif in view of the extreme emphasis and ritual description given to the betrothal of Cúchulainn and Emer. There need be no actual childbirth for a royal (god-like) marriage to be symbolic of fertility. Zeus certainly is not notable for his children *within* marriage, and the same can be said of Odin.

replication of a mythic pattern under changed circumstances—a common state of affairs in early literature. The existence of these patterns demonstrates the antiquity of the source material available to the compiler of the *Cattle Raid of Cooley*, but does not provide enough of a straight-jacket to have prevented strange mixings and mis-applications on his part. The " Boyhood Deeds " have meaning, are where they are because they belong there in terms of an existing pattern, and have parallels elsewhere in early Indo-European literature. The fact that they seem rather arbitrarily connected to the rest of the saga should not blind us to these important facts.

There is strong evidence that the " Boyhood Deeds " must be in origin one of the most archaic parts of the *Cattle Raid of Cooley*, that Versions A and B are parallel narrative equivalents of each other, that this parallelism is an example of the kind of multiformity more characteristic of oral than of written tradition, and that the evidence here for an updated multiform text of a single archaic incident group is a further indication that one of the strongest forces operating on the tradition of this important saga was the introduction of variants.

If Versions A and B of the " Boyhood Deeds " did in fact exist in multiform close to the time of compilation of the earlier version of the *Cattle Raid of Cooley*, this fact may help to account for the " modernity " noted by Carney and others, for if conflation of an existing multiform tradition of the story was a recent event, there is no reason why some " improvement " might not have been attempted. In addition to the above conclusions, these tales illustrate the ways in which story patterning exists on levels beyond the semantic ones of " formula " and the narrative ones of " theme " ; the process of building and manipulating concrete metaphors pervades early literature to an extent we find hard to comprehend in the milieu of modern psychological fiction.

DANIEL F. MELIA

*University of California, Berkeley*

APPENDIX A

The incidents in both versions of the " Boyhood Deeds " are quite discrete and easily summarized in general ; in LU there are even scribal titles for most of the incidents. The incident divisions shown here are part of a more elaborate division of the entire *Cattle Raid of Cooley*. For a theoretical justification of the methodology see my unpub. diss. One interesting note is that one of the titles given by " M ", the main hand of LU, to one of the divisions of Version B of the " Boyhood Deeds ", " *Aided na Macraide inso* " (" This is the death of the boytroop ") [LU 4912], is repeated at the head of a similar incident later in the saga [LU 5904], interpolated by a later hand, " H ", providing a further small piece of evidence for some kind of thematic composition.

From the *Book of Leinster* [LL], lines 738-1217: Version A.
  I.  1. Cúchulainn (Sétanta) hears stories of the Ulster court.
      2. He asks his parents' permission to go, but is refused (because he is only seven.)
      3. He goes anyway, carrying his stick and ball.
      4. He meets the boytroop of Ulster and defeats them in a game.

5. They attack him as an outsider because he has not asked for their legal protection.
6. He runs to his uncle, King Conchobor, and identifies himself.
7. The boytroop then accepts him, but he attacks *them*.
8. They ask *his* protection, which he grants.

II. 1. Sétanta (while playing) hears of Culann the Smith's feast from Conchobor.
2. He promises to come later when he has finished his game.
3. Conchobor arrives at the feast, forgets the lad, and tells Culann that no one else is coming.
4. Culann lets his fierce hound loose.
5. Sétanta heads for the feast with his toys.
6. He is attacked by the hound.
7. He kills the hound (with his bare hands and his toys.)
8. He is reproached by Culann.
9. He offers himself as a substitute hound.
10. He tries to refuse his new name, Cú Chulainn ["Hound of Culann"].
11. He finally accepts his new name under pressure from the older men.

III. 1. Cathbad, the druid, tells his students that the day is auspicious for taking arms.
2. Cúchulainn overhears him.
3. Cúchulainn goes to King Conchobor to ask for arms.
4. Conchobor questions him.
5. Conchobor gives in when told that Cathbad has advised it.
6. Cúchulainn repeatedly breaks ordinary arms.
7. Conchobor gives his nephew his own (Conchobor's) arms.
8. Cathbad enters and denies having advised Cúchulainn.
9. Cúchulainn explains and asks acceptance of his decision.
10. Conchobor accepts it.
11. Cúchulainn breaks several chariots.
12. Conchobor's own chariot finally stands up to Cúchulainn.

IV. 1. (On Cúchulainn's inaugural chariot ride) Ibar, the charioteer, suggests that they return to the court at Emain Macha.
2. Cúchulainn makes him go around Emain.
3. Ibar again urges that they return.
4. Cúchulainn again refuses.
5. The boytroop scolds him for leaving so soon.
6. Ibar again tries to get the horses back to pasture.
7. They then go to *Ath na Foraire* ("the Ford of the Sentry-Post") as Cúchulainn learns local topographic lore from the charioteer.
8. Cúchulainn wants to keep watch on the border.
9. He is rebuffed by the hero Conall Cernach because of his youth.
10. Cúchulainn says he will kill someone to prove himself.
11. Conall wants to come to protect him.
12. Cúchulainn breaks the yoke of Conall's chariot.
13. Conall returns to *Ath na Foraire*.

V. 1. Cúchulainn goes south.
2. He asks Ibar to explain the territory.
3. Cúchulainn wants to go to the stronghold of the three sons of Nechta.
4. Ibar tries to dissuade him.
5. Cúchulainn insists on going anyway.
6. Cúchulainn challenges the three sons of Nechta. (They must come from a distance.)
7. Cúchulainn wants to sleep in the chariot.
8. Ibar tries to dissuade him.
9. Foill, the first son, appears and asks who is there.
10. He refuses to fight Cúchulainn because he is too young.
11. Cúchulainn challenges Foill again.
12. Ibar again warns Cúchulainn.
13. Cúchulainn kills Foill with the *deil cliss* (a magic weapon.)
14. Tuachell (brother no. 2) comes and accepts the challenge with taunts.
15. Ibar warns Cúchulainn yet again.
16. Cúchulainn kills Tuachell with Conchobor's lance.

17. Faindle (no. 3) appears and challenges Cúchulainn to fight in the ford.
18. Ibar warns Cúchulainn.
19. Cúchulainn kills Faindle with Conchobor's sword.
20. They destroy the fort and return to Emain.

VI. 1. Cúchulainn asks Ibar whether it is better to kill or capture some deer he sees, and Ibar advises capture as a more worthy feat.
2. Conchobor's horses fail Cúchulainn.
3. He catches the deer on foot.
4. He asks Ibar the same question about some swans and gets the same reply.
5. He knocks the birds down with a slingshot.
6. He makes Ibar collect the birds from the moving chariot while he (Cúchulainn) drives.

VII. 1. Cúchulainn and the charioteer go to Emain and are described arriving by the seeress, Leborcham.
2. She prophesies that he will kill the Ulstermen in his frenzy.
3. Conchobor then identifies him and agrees.
4. They send naked women to meet him.
5. He hides his face, is taken and put in three successive vats of water. The first one bursts, the second boils away, and the third cools him down.
6. Finally calmed, he is clothed.
7. He is placed at Conchobor's side.

From the *Book of the Dun Cow* [LU], lines 4855-5210: Versions A and B.
I. Essentially identical in structure to LL incident I. above.

II. 1. Cúchulainn will not sleep.
2. When asked why, he demands a pillar-stone at his head and feet.
3. This request is granted.

III. 1. A man tries to awaken Cúchulainn.
2. He dashes the man's brains out.
3. " No one ever tried that again."

IV. 1. Cúchulainn is playing with the boytroop.
2. He accidentally kills fifty of them.
3. He runs to Conchobor's bedchamber.
4. Fergus makes peace between Cúchulainn and the boytroop. [Fergus is a kind of Chief of Staff at Emain, a former king, and Cúchulainn's foster father.]

VERSION B

V. 1. The Ulstermen go to battle against Eoghan mac Durthacht while Cúchulainn is left at home asleep (see III, 3 above).
2. The Ulstermen are defeated.
3. Cúchulainn hears the groans of Conchobor and others and awakens (breaking the pillar-stones as he gets up).
4. Cúchulainn meets Fergus at the door of the fort, wounded, and asks him where everyone is, but Fergus does not know.
5. Cúchulainn goes out and sees a man with half a head carrying half a man on his back.
6. The carrier asks Cúchulainn for help.
7. Cúchulainn refuses [perhaps because the man is an otherworld being.]
8. They fight and Cúchulainn is thrown.
9. The Badb [a war goddess] appears and taunts Cúchulainn.
10. Cúchulainn revives and wins.
11. Cúchulainn calls Conchobor, finds him, and lifts him from a trench.
12. Cúchulainn goes in search of a roast pig that Conchobor has requested to revive him.
13. He kills a warrior who is cooking a pig and brings it back.
14. Conchobor eats the pig and revives.
15. Cúchulainn goes back to Emain carrying Conchobor and picks up Cuscraid, one of Conchobor's sons, on the way as well.

VI. 1. The Ulstermen are in the *cés noinden* [a mysterious nine-day debility with which they were afflicted from time to time].
  2. Three nines of the men of Faiche attack Emain. The women scream.
  3. The boytroop hears the screams and begins to come to help.
  4. All finally run away except Cúchulainn. [He is exempt from the *cés noinden* because he is only half Ulsterman.]
  5. Cúchulainn kills nine of the men and chases the rest away, but sustains severe wounds.

VII. Essentially identical in structure with LL II.
VIII. Essentially identical in structure with LL III.
IX. Essentially identical in structure with LL IV.
X. Essentially identical with LL V. except the plundering of the fort is not mentioned.
XI. Essentially the same as LL VI.
XII. Essentially identical with LL VII.

# CAEDMON AS A FORMULAIC POET*

" The later skalds have composed after the example of the old skalds."
Snorri *Edda* II.33

Four scenes illustrate unquestionably oral composition of poetry in the Anglo-Saxon context:

*Beowulf* lines 853-917 (horseback praise of Beowulf)[1]
*Beowulf* lines 2105-2114 (Hroðgar's remembrances)
*Egil's Saga* chapters 59-60 (the " head song ")[2]
Bede's *Ecclesiastical History* IV. 24 (Caedmon).[3]

But in the corpus of about 30,000 lines, only *Caedmon's Hymn* can confidently be called oral. The only other poem for which we have a descriptive context indicating any possibility of oral composition, Bede's *Death Song*, may have been written ahead of time and recited from memory.[4] Bede, like most hagiographers, had an eye for a good death scene, and probably prepared his own carefully. F. P. Magoun's seminal 1953 article " Oral-Formulaic Character of Anglo-Saxon Narrative Poetry ",[5] applied Milman Parry's notion that formulas in early poetry indicate oral composition, to Old English ; but in 1966, Larry Benson exploded the necessary identification of formularity and orality.[6] Since then, a consensus seems to be emerging that written Old English poetry used oral forms, but no reliable test can differentiate written from oral poems.[7]

---

* *Caedmon's Hymn* scholarship owes much to the late E. V. K. Dobbie, and I dedicate this paper to his memory.

[1] All Old English poetic references from G. P. Krapp and E. V. K. Dobbie, eds., *Anglo-Saxon Poetic Records*, 6 vols., (New York: Columbia U.P., 1931-1953).

[2] Gwyn Jones, trans., *Egil's Saga* (Syracuse: Syracuse Univ. Press, 1960), pp. 154-165. See discussion in F. P. Magoun, " Bede's Story of Caedman: The Case History of an Anglo-Saxon Oral Singer ", *Speculum*, 30 (1955), 59-60, n. 23 (hereafter cited as " Caedman "), and Lars Lönnroth, " Hjálmar's Death-Song and the Delivery of Eddic Poetry ", *Speculum*, 46 (1971), 3.

[3] Unless otherwise specified, all references to the Latin version from B. Colgrave and R. A. B. Mynors, eds., and trans., *Bede's Ecclesiastical History of the English People* (Oxford: Oxford Univ. Press, 1969), hereafter cited as " *H.E.*"

[4] All references to Cuthbert's *Epistola de Obitu Bedae* from Colgrave and Mynors, pp. 580-587. Cf. Charles Plummer, ed. *Venerabilis Baedae Opera Historica* (Oxford: Oxford U.P., 1896), I, clx-clxiv, lxi-lxxviii, hereafter cited as " Plummer " ; and E. V. K. Dobbie, *The Manuscripts of Caedmon's Hymn and Bede's Death Song* (New York : Columbia U.P., 1937), especially 49 ff. W. Bulst, " Bedas Sterbelied ", *ZfdA*, 75 (1938), 111-114 attributes the death song to Caedmon.

[5] *Speculum*, 28 (1953), 446-463, repr. in my *Beowulf Poet* (Englewood Cliffs, N.J.: Prentice-Hall, 1968), 83—113, hereafter cited as " Character ".

[6] " The Literary Character of Anglo-Saxon Formulaic Poetry ", *PMLA*, 81 (1966), 334-341.

[7] A. C. Watts, *The Lyre and the Harp* (New Haven and London: Yale U.P., 1969) ; R. F. Lawrence, " The Formulaic Theory and its Application to English Alliterative Poetry ", in R. Fowler, ed., *Essays on Style and Language* (New York: Humanities Press, 1966), 166-183.

In this paper, I shall re-examine Bede's story of Caedmon to highlight certain details, especially differences in the Latin and Old English versions, and to attempt to explain the miracle. Then I shall examine Magoun's analytical method and provide an alternative of my own in order to explain the genesis of Caedmon's diction and of Old English Christian poetic diction.

# I

Caedmon's story appears in Bede's *Ecclesiastical History*, which survives in its original Latin and in an Old English translation. About 162 copies or fragments of the Latin version exist, of which twelve contain *Caedmon's Hymn* in Old English, the earliest of this sub-category being Cambridge University Library Ms. Kk.V.16, the so-called "Moore Manuscript", dated from internal evidence to 737.[8] The Old English translation, done by King Alfred or at his behest, survives in five manuscripts, ranging from the tenth to the middle of the eleventh centuries.[9] Bede records the hymn only in a Latin paraphrase, but twelve later scribes added the Old English version in the margins, integrated into the text, or at the end.[10]

Some details in the story illuminate problems in the formulaic theory. First, Cynewulf has been presumed literate because he uses and even translates Latin sources in his poetry. But Caedmon, though presumably illiterate, could and did incorporate scholarly materials into his poems:

> ita ut, quicquid ex diuinis litteris per interpretes disceret, hoc ipse post pusillum, uerbis poeticis maxima suauitate et conpunctione conpositis in sua, id est Anglorum, lingua proferret.

[8] Colgrave and Mynors, xxxix-lxxvi ; the manuscripts are:
Bd Bodleian Ms Bodley 163.
Di Dijon, Bibliothèque Municipale Ms 574.
H Bodleian Ms Hatton 43.
Hr Hereford Cathedral Library Ms P.5.1.
L Leningrad Public Library Ms Lat. Q.v.I.18.
Ld₁ Bodleian Ms Laud Misc. 243.
Ln Lincoln College Oxford Ms Lat 31.
M Cambrige Univ. Library Ms Kk.v.16.
Mg Magdalen College Oxford Ms 105.
P₁ Paris, Bibliothèque Nationale Codex Lat. 5237.
Tr₁ Trinity College Cambridge Ms R.5.22.
W Winchester Cathedral Library Ms 1 (or 3).
Cf. Dobbie, 11-22, 34-42.

[9] Dobbie, 22-28 ; all references to the Old English version from T. Miller, ed. and trans., *The Old English Version of Bede's Ecclesiastical History*, EETS OS 95-96, 110-111 (Oxford U.P., 1890-1891, 1898 ; repr. 1959-1963). The manuscripts are:
B₁ Corpus Christi College Cambridge Ms 41.
C British Museum Cotton Otho B.XI.
Ca Cambridge Univ. Library Ms Kk.III.18.
O Corpus Christi College Oxford Ms 279.
Tr Bodleian Ms Tanner 10.

[10] Dobbie, 11-43, and M. G. Frampton, "*Caedmon's Hymn*", *MP*, 22 (1924), 1-15. On the question of the Old English text as a back translation from the Latin, see J. J. Conybeare, *Illustrations of Anglo-Saxon Poetry* (London, 1826), p. 7 ; R. Wülcker, "Über den Hymnus Caedmons", *BGDSL*, 3 (1876), 348-357 ; Dobbie, 47 ; J. Zupitza, "Über den Hymnus Cädmons", *ZfdA*, 22 (1878), 210-223 ; A. H. Smith, ed., *Three Northumbrian Poems* (London: Methuen, corrected ed., 1968), 12 ff., hereafter cited as "3NP."

(Page 414: thus, whatever he learned from the holy Scriptures by means of interpreters, he quickly turned into extremely delightful and moving poetry, in English, which was his own tongue.)[11]

Latin *interpretes* may mean "translators" as well as "explainers" ; there is no evidence that Caedmon ever knew any Latin. Again,

exponebantque illi quendam sacrae historiae siue doctrinae sermonem, praecipientes eum, si posset, hunc in modulationem carminis transferre. At ille suscepto negotio abiit, et mane rediens optimo carmine quod iubebatur conpositum reddidit.

(418: They then read to him a passage of sacred history or doctrine, bidding him make a song out of it, if he could, in metrical form. He undertook the task and went away ; on returning next morning he repeated the passage he had been given, which he had put into excellent verse.)

The Old English translator, like most Old English translators, paraphrases rather than converting verbatim ;[12] he renders the Latin:

þa rehton hei him 7 sægdon sum halig spell 7 godcundre lare word: bebudon him þa, gif he meahte, þæt he in swinsunge leoþsonges þæt gehwyrfde. þa he ða hæfde þa wisan onfongne, þa eode he ham to his huse ; 7 cwom eft on morgenne, 7 þy betstan leoðe geglenged him asong 7 ageaf, þæt him beboden wæs.

(344: Then they recited and said to him a certain holy narrative and words of sacred doctrine ; then they directed him, if he could, that he should turn that into harmony of verse-song. When he had taken on the task, he went home to his house ; and he came again in the morning, he sang and gave them in the best composed verse what had been directed for him.)

Note the difference in " sacrae historiae *siue* doctrinae sermonem " and " halig spell 7 godcundre lare word ". The Latin implies Caedmon's close adherence to his given passage ; he repeats (*reddidit*) history *or* doctrine turned into verse. The Old English version's *and* (7) implies that he combined history *and* doctrine. The first technique coincides to a certain extent with what we call " Caedmonian " verse, the second with " Cynewulfian ", where the doctrinal portion of the poem remains more prominent, less integrated under the narrative surface. It would be possible, although improbable, that poets could even translate Latin orally by dictation, whether they were able to write or not. Charlemagne spoke fluent Latin, read Greek, and studied grammar, rhetoric, and dialectic. Yet Einhard says, " He also tried to write, and used to keep tablets and blanks in bed under his pillow, that at leisure hours he might accustom his hand to form the letters ; however, as he did not begin his efforts in due season, but late in life, they met with ill success ".[13] At the other end of literacy, Bede on his deathbed dictated the ending of his translation of John 1:1-6:9 and of Isidore's *Liber*

---

[11] Page numbers from Colgrave and Mynors for the Latin, Miller for the Old English ; Old English translations are mine.

[12] F. A. Payne, *King Alfred and Boethius* (Madison: Univ. of Wisconsin Press, 1968).

[13] Einhard, *The Life of Charlemagne*, trans. S. E. Turner (Ann Arbor: Univ. of Michigan Press, 1960), p. 54.

*Rotarum* to a scribe.[14] In the First Bible of Charles the Bald, folio 3 verso shows Jerome dictating his translation of the Bible ; whether he actually dictated it or not, some illuminator *circa* 846 thought he could.[15] In short, Cynewulf's poetry and even *Metres of Boethius* could be works produced without writing, although probability and simple ease would argue the contrary.[16]

Improvisation remains a keystone of formulaic theory as well as one of its major stumbling blocks ; most modern critics find the subtleties of *Beowulf* or *Elene* too profound for extemporizing. Bede's story supports their skepticism, for, with the exception of the original hymn recited to the visitor in a dream, Caedmon awake never extemporizes. Three examples illustrate his pre-performance care and planning:

1. Exsurgens autem a somno, cuncta quae dormiens cantauerat memoriter retenuit, et eis mox plura in eundem modum uerba Deo digni carminis adiunxit.

   (416: When he awoke, he remembered all that he had sung while asleep and soon added more verses in the same manner, praising God in fitting style.)

2. [The passage quoted above where Caedmon passes the test of turning history and/or doctrine into verse overnight.]

3. At ipse cuncta, quae audiendo discere poterat, rememorando secum et quasi mundum animal ruminando, in carmen dulcissimum conuertebat.

   (418: He learned all he could by listening to them and then, memorizing it and ruminating over it, like some clean animal chewing the cud, he turned it into the most melodious verse.)

In the first passage, Caedmon adds to the hymn after he awakens ; despite Bede's failure to record these additional verses, we may assume that Caedmon recited them in the morning. His first performance showed practice, and perhaps he even polished the original hymn. The second passage involves the same overnight preparation. The third passage implies, by its imagery of a cow slowly chewing her cud, careful and private composition before performance. Magoun interprets these passages as revealing Caedmon's status as a beginner: " Here his procedure was perhaps that of a not very experienced singer, at least as far as public performances were concerned. . . . Such an [overnight] interval between mastering the narrative material and a performance before an audience is apt to characterize either an inexperienced singer or a perfectionist " (Caedman, 59-60). But Bede indicates no change or improvement upon this original procedure as Caedmon gained experience ; Magoun, writing in 1955, was perhaps too influenced by the Yugoslav parallel to admit alternatives to improvisation. In some cultures,

---

[14] Cuthbert's *Epistola*, 582-585.

[15] Bibliothèque Nationale Ms Lat. I, fol. 3v, in J. Hubert, J. Porcher, and W. F. Volbach, *The Carolingian Renaissance* (New York: Braziller, 1970), plate 126, p. 137.

[16] Magoun Caedman, 60-61 ; Benson, 337-341 ; Watts, 188-193 ; and W. Whallon, *Formula, Character, and Context* (Cambridge: Harvard U.P., 1969), 208-210.

moreover, improvisation and prior composition co-exist. Magoun footnotes the passage above with a reference to Egil's " head-song ", a twenty verse *drápa* composed overnight to save the hero from Erik Bloodaxe's wrath. Egil composes this medium-length poem orally and memorizes it for delivery, just as Bragi evidently had done before to save himself from the Swedish king Björn (*Egil's Saga*, ch. 59) ; but throughout this saga we see Egil tossing off verses extemporaneously. Further, modern Somali oral poets face highly critical audiences, and " aware of this, most poets, except for a few of real genius, do not put their trust in improvisation, but spend many hours, sometimes even days, composing their works ".[17] Improvisation was evidently not Caedmon's style ; indeed, I find no evidence of any extemporizing poet in Old English.

Transmission of oral poems continues to vex scholars. Homer seems to have composed before writing began, or was used for extended literary purposes, yet his poems survived. Memorization accounts for this phenomenon well enough, particularly considering the fabulous memories of some cultures. Xenophon gives this vignette:

" My father was anxious to see me develop into a good man," said Niceratus, " and as a means to this end he compelled me to memorize all of Homer ; and so even now I can repeat the whole *Iliad* and the *Odyssey* by heart."

" But have you failed to observe," questioned Antisthenes, " that the rhapsodes, too, all know these poems "

" How could I," he replied, " when I listen to their recitations nearly every day? "

" Well, do you know any tribe of men," went on the other, " more stupid than the rhapsodes? "[18]

No one expresses surprise at Niceratus's feat. Andrzejewski reports that Somali poets memorize long poems, build huge repertoires, " can learn a poem by heart after hearing it only once ", and have illiterate audiences arguing later over the purity of textual readings (*Somali Poetry*, 45-46). King Alfred, according to his biographer Asser, memorized recited Saxon poems.[19] Memorization of long works was possible,[20] and Caedmon probably recorded his poems by dictation for subsequent memorization. Bede tells us only that " suauiusque resonando doctores suos uicossim auditores sui faciebat " (418: and it sounded so sweet as he recited it that his teachers

[17] B. W. Andrzejewski and I. M. Lewis, *Somali Poetry* (Oxford U.P., 1964), 45. Cf. Alan Jabbour, " Memorial Transmission in Old English Poetry ", *Chaucer Review*, 3 (1969), 174-190 ; J. Opland, " ' Scop ' and ' Imbongi ': Anglo-Saxon and Banto Oral Poets ", *ESA*, 14 (1971) 161-178.

[18] Xenophon, *Symposium and Apology*, ed. and trans., O. J. Todd (Cambridge: Harvard U.P., 1947), III, 5-6, p. 405.

[19] W. H. Stevenson, ed., *Asser's Life of King Alfred* (Oxford U.P., new impression with additions, 1959), pp. 20 and 221-225. Cf. C. Plummer, *Life and Times of Alfred the Great* (Oxford U.P., 1902), pp. 81-83 ; W. A. Chaney, *The Cult of Kingship in Anglo-Saxon England* (Berkeley: Univ. of California Press, 1970), pp. 175-176 ; and D. Bethurum, " Stylistic Features of the Old English Laws ", *MLR*, 27 (1932), 264-279.

[20] But see Caedman, 53, 59-60 ; Jabbour op. cit. ; and Lönnroth, 18.

became in turn his audience), which the translator modifies to " þætte seolfan þa his lareowas æt his muðe wreoton 7 leornodon " (346: that his own teachers themselves wrote them down from his mouth and learned them). Regardless of the translator's accuracy about this dictation and memorization in Caedmon's practice, we can say that a ninth century writer believed in this process of memory producing dictated works which were in turn memorized.

Our rational age must inevitably question this miraculous gift of song ; indeed, Sir Frances Palgrave, followed by many early critics, believed the whole story fictitious.[21] That this particular miracle has wide currency as a folklore motif in Greek, Norse, Old Saxon, etc. need not lead us to doubt it or its details.[22] Magoun explains the miracle as the overcoming of stage fright: Caedmon had surely heard songs ; " one might suspect that Caedmon occasionally sang when alone or thought he was alone, say, when out in the fields tending his flock and that on one or more occasions he had been over-heard " ; friends therefore called on him ; and eventually the dream over-came his shyness (Caedman, 58-59). Magoun assumes the necessity of pre-Caedmonian Christian vernacular poetry in England: " much points to an early development of a supplementary diction making possible formulaic reference to the Deity and other characteristically Christian matters and consequently it is to be supposed that Caedman had heard and learned enough of these to be sufficient to his purpose in the *Hymn* and subsequent songs " (Caedman, 58). He notes the possibility of Aldhelm's singing religious songs on his famous bridge. William of Malmesbury concludes: " Hoc com-mento sensim inter ludicra verbis Scripturarum insertis, cives ad sanitatem reduxisse ", which Magoun translates: " By this device, gradually working in words of the Scriptures among entertaining words, he led the people back to right reason ".[23] Whallon translates: " and would compose poetry in which words from the Scriptures were combined with more popular matters " (Whallon, 130). Whether this passage means Aldhelm used Christian diction in vernacular poetry or that he recited secular poems as bait and switched to Christian preaching separately remains uncertain, but this passage con-tains the only known reference to possible pre-Caedmonian Christian ver-nacular poetic diction. Bede, on the other hand, implies that Caedmon

---

[21] " Observations on the History of Caedmon ", *Archaeologia*, 24 (1832), 341-343. But see E. Sievers, ed., *Heliand* (Halle, 1878), 3 ff. ; Plummer, II, 255 ; and 3NP, 12-14. Further references in L. Pound, " Caedmon's Dream Song ", in *Studies in English Philology, A Miscellany in Honor of Frederick Klaeber*, ed. K. Malone and M. B. Ruud (Univ. of Minnesota Press, 1929), 232-239.

[22] For examples see Pound, op. cit. and 3NP 14 ; also Caedman, 58, n. 21 and D. W. Fritz, " Caedmon: A Traditional Christian Poet ", MS, 31 (1969), 334—37. The best introduction to poetic inspiration is Alice Sperduti Wilson, " The Divine Nature of Poetry in Antiquity ", *TAPA*, 81 (1950), 209-240.

[23] William of Malmesbury, *De Gestis Pontificum Anglorum*, ed. N. E. S. A. Hamilton (London: H.M.S.O., 1870), 336 ; trans. Magoun Character, 454-455, n. 16. Cf. K. Malone, " Caedmon and English Poetry ", MLN, 76 (1961), 193-195 and N. F. Blake, " Caed-mon's Hymn ", N & Q, 207 (1962), 243-246.

began the tradition:

Et quidem et alii post illum in gente Anglorum religiosa poemata facere temtabant, sed nullus eum aequiperare potuit.
(414: It is true that after him other Englishmen attempted to compose religious poems, but none could compare with him.)
Ond eac swelce monige oðre æfter him in Ongelþeode ongunnon æfeste leoð wyrcan: ac nænig hwæðre him þæt gelice don meahte.
(342: And also many others after him among the English-people tried [or began] to make religious poems ; however, no one could do that like him.)

As opposed to Magoun's notion of Caedmon as a closet *scop*, I prefer to explain the miracle in terms of unconscious absorption of formulaic diction. Magoun notes that Caedmon had probably heard singing all his long life (Caedman, 56). Indeed, sung narratives seem to have formed the main entertainment of all levels of Anglo-Saxon society from king (*Beowulf* 2105-2114) to cowherd (Caedmon's *gebeorscipe*) ; and J. Opland goes so far as to say that " it seems likely that in Anglo-Saxon times all men could and did sing in the traditional manner " (Opland, 176). Albert Lord discerns three stages in a singer's arrival as a performer: 1. listening, 2. singing to himself, 3. public performance.[24] The listening stage proceeds like this:

During the first period he sits aside while others sing. He has decided that he wants to sing himself, or he may still be unaware of this decision and simply be very eager to hear the stories of his elders. Before he actually begins to sing, he is, consciously or unconsciously, laying the foundation. He is learning the stories and becoming acquainted with the heroes and their names, the faraway places and the habits of long ago. The themes of the poetry are becoming familiar to him, and his feeling for them is sharpened as he hears more and as he listens to the men discussing the songs among themselves. At the same time he is imbibing the rhythm of the singing and to an extent also the rhythms of the thoughts as they are expressed in song. Even at this early stage the oft-repeated phrases which we call formulas are being absorbed (Lord, 21).

Caedmon probably knew the formulas, systems, themes, and type-scenes from listening to them. The second stage coincides with Caedmon's dream and his practice as he adds other verses through the night. Stage three is the recitation for Abbess Hild and the scholars. Stage one probably took longer than normal for Yugoslav singers, while two and three happen perhaps too fast for the Serbo-Croatian analogy. But then Caedmon did feel divinely inspired, and the abbess commanded (*het*) him to perform.

One might object (as Magoun does, 57-58) that formulaic diction develops very slowly, whereas Caedmon uses phrases seemingly fresh-coined, such as *heofonrices weard* and *ece Drihten*. Bede says Caedmon " coepit cantare in laudem Dei Conditoris uersus quos nunquam audierat " (416: began to sing verses which he had never heard before in praise of God the Creator), which the translator renders: " ongan he . . . singan in herenesse Godes Scyppendes

[24] *The Singer of Tales* (Cambridge: Harvard Univ. Press, 1960), chap. 2.

þa fers 7 *þa word* þe he næfre gehyrde" (344: he began to sing in praise of God the Shaper verses *and words* which he had never heard [my italics]). Perhaps Bede thought of this new creation of formulaic diction as part of the miracle. Or perhaps Caedmon converted pre-Christian formulas for pagan deities into phrases praising his God ; *frea ælmihtig* could apply just as well to Odin as to Jehovah.[25] Furthermore, life copies art; phrases from our literature pervade our daily thoughts. In a society devoted to oral poetry, Caedmon would carry thousands of epithets for heros and gods in his head. I can easily imagine such a pious man mentally doodling with popular formulas, idly applying them to the God he worshipped. *Meotodes meahte* easily applies to Odin: *ece Drihten* less so. Perhaps Caedmon incorporated some pagan epithets by merely capitalizing the nouns for deity ; others he modified, as easily as filling the system " (adjec'tive) Drih'ten ",† a source of useful phrases for describing princes, with the adjective *ece*. Caedmon had it all in his head, and his dream launched his singing career.

## II

In this section, I shall discuss Magoun's analysis of the diction of *Caedmon's Hymn* and propose an alternative model. Magoun used Parry's coded system of underlining to analyze formulas and systems:

> The late Milman Parry defined a poetical formula as " a group of words which is regularly employed under the same metrical conditions to express a given essential idea " and these are marked on the Chart . . . by solid underlining. As for systems of formulas he writes: " any group of two or more such like formulas makes up a system, and the system may be defined in turn as a group of phrases which have the same metrical value and which are enough alike in thought and words to leave no doubt that the poet who used them knew then not only as a single formula, but also as formulas of a certain type." The latter are marked on the Chart by broken underlining. Following the marked text comes the supporting evidence, *i.e.*, instances of verses of the *Hymn* recurring elsewhere in the Anglo-Saxon poetical corpus (Caedman, 53).

His analysis of *Caedmon's Hymn*, given in his normalized orthography, follows:

## CHART

Nū wē sculon herian    heofon-rīces Weard,

Metodes meahte    and His mōd-ȝeþanc,

weorc Wuldor-fæder,    swā hē wundra gehwæs,

ōece Dryhten,    ōr (var. ord) onstealde.

† For technical reasons, here and throughout this article, the signs ' and " are used to indicate primary and secondary stress respectively.

[25] Whallon, 138 and his " Idea of God in *Beowulf* ", *PMLA*, 80 (1965), 19-23; Watts, 147.

5 Hē āerest (ȝe)scōp ielda (var. eorðan) bearnum

heofon to hrōfe hāliȝ Scieppend ;

þā middan-ȝeard mann-cynnes Weard,

ōece Dryhten æfter tēode—

fīrum foldan Frēa eall-mihtiȝ.

(Caedman, 62).

He gives thirty lines of " Supporting Evidence ", too long to quote beyond this example: " 1a *Gen* 816 Nū mē mæȝ hrēowan ; *And* 1517 Nū þū meaht ȝecnāwan ; *Ele* 511 Nū þū meaht gehīeran ; *Bwf* 395 Nū ȝē moton gangan " (Caedman, 62). No supporting evidence appears for verses 6a and 9a. I feel this underlining method prevents us from seeing the poet at work in the language. It is mechanical to a fault, and probably accounts for some of the hostility felt by opponents of the formulaic school.[26] It also fails to account for some verses, not just 6a and 9a, but even 1a. The fact that four half-lines in *Genesis, Andreas, Elene,* and *Beowulf* begin with *Nu* tells us very little about the poet's schematized diction, indeed almost nothing beyond the fact that *Nu* did begin verses. Although he underlines solidly the pronoun *we,* he cites no supporting evidence for it in that position. The broken underlining under *sculon herian* indicates a system, but from his supporting evidence, we could only propose " *Nu'* (auxiliary verb) (infi'nitive) ", not a system by Parry's definition. But, Magoun, pioneering in 1955, did not have the benefit of almost two decades of scholarship which has tended to modify his notion of repetition as the essence of the formula.[27] Magoun's underlining records only repetitions and seeks to produce a statistical base for measuring formularity, predicated on the axiom that a high percentage of formulas indicates oral composition.

In my article " Old English Formulas and Systems ",[28] I proposed two new definitions, with the system as generator of formulas: " A system in Old English formulaic poetry may be defined as a group of half-lines, usually loosely related metrically and semantically, which are related in form by the identical relative placement of two elements, one a variable word or element of a compound usually supplying the alliteration, and the other a constant word or element of a compound, with approximately the same distribution of non-stressed elements " (OEFS, 203). The formula is " a group of words, one half-line in length, which shows evidence of being the direct product of a formulaic system " (OEFS, 204). In my sequel article, I added that

[26] Whallon, 73 calls it unreliable, undiscriminating, and unanalytical, while Watts, 150-151 rightly traces the mechanical side of it to Parry.

[27] Watts, 68-70 and references in her footnotes.

[28] *English Studies,* 48 (1967), 193-204, hereafter cited as " OEFS ", and my sequel article " Some Aesthetic Implications of a New Definition of the Formula ", *NM,* 69 (1968), 516-522. These definitions owe much to Wayne O'Neil, " Oral-Formulaic Structure in Old English Elegaic Poetry ", unpublished Ph.D. diss., Univ. of Wisconsin, 1960, *DA,* 31 (1960), 625. For recent definitions, see Whallon, 74 and Watts, 90.

50

" systems remove the necessity for verbatim repetition since we only need find another similar verse from which the system can be abstracted. . . . The poet can, of course, inflect (or gradate) any of the words in the system, and the nonstressed words, especially particles, are immaterial. In some cases, the constant element already alliterates, so that the poet need not supply an alliterating variable " (Implications, 518-519). The essence of this definition lies in the idea of systems as a pool of organized diction. If a poet knows an extant verse which already fits his exact requirements in terms of alliteration, esthetics, and meaning, he incorporates it whole. If it needs slight modification, he changes it within limits. If he remembers no such verse, the diction organized into systems will generate one for him. Now let us analyze *Caedmon's Hymn* into systems by these definitions.[29]

1a *Nu sculon herian*: Justice Holmes said: " Hard cases make bad law " ; verse 1a, a tough one, must await later treatment.

1b *heofonrices weard*: Easy cases make scholarship deceptively simple ; this verse occurs verbatim twenty-two other times in the corpus, e.g.:

1. *And* 52: herede in heortan   heofonrices weard
2. *Gen* 1363: Him on hoh beleac   heofonrices weard
3. *XSt* 420: Nu ic þe halsige,   heofenrices weard.[30]

Even if it had not been repeated, we could use the following to establish its system:

1. *Chr* 1527: Biõ þonne rices weard   reþe ond meahtig
2. *Jud* 80: swiõran folme ;   ongan õa swegles weard
3. *Mnl* 210: upengla weard.   þænne embe eahta niht
4. *Rdl* 13.7: reafe birofene,   rodra weardes

(The *rice* in #1 is heaven.) In each, *weard* occupies the second stress with an alliterating word preceding it, and the alliterating words mean the same as *heofonrices*, even in the same genitive case. The system could be written in its barest form " $(X')$ wea'rd ", X meaning the substituted element, and italics for alliteration. Or it could be more detailed: " *(genitive nou'n)* wea'rd ". Notice that the unstressed elements and inflections of *weard-* may vary. More examples imply a possibly more complex system:

1. *Bwf* 1390: Aris, rices weard,   uton raþe feran
2. *Dan* 176: for þam þe gleaw ne wæs,   gumrices weard
3. *Aza* 107: blace, breahtumhwate   brytenrices weard,

which might be written " $(X')$-rices wea'rd." The first two refer to earthly rulers ; all three may antedate Caedmon as epithets for kings.[31] These examples could antedate him too and could have applied to pagan gods:

1. *Chr* 243: sweotule geseþan. Cum, nu, sigores weard

[29] I use the West Saxon version to avoid confusion when dealing with parallel verses, mostly in the same dialect.

[30] Also in *And* 56, *Dan* 12, 26, *DrR* 91, *Ele* 197, 445, 718, *Exo* 486, *Gen* 1484, 1744, 2073, *Glc* 611, 789, *JgD* 2.70, *KtH* 2, *MBo* 11.31, *Mnl* 4, *Ps* 50.113, *PPs* 90.1.2 ; abbreviations from *ÉA*, 8 (1955), 138-146, all essentially phonetic.

[31] See also *Bwf* 921, 2513, 2580, 3066, *Ele* 153, *LPr* 3.19.

2. *Dan* 596: middangeardes weard, ac his mod astah

3. *Exo* 504: þæt wæs mihtigra mereflodes weard.

Caedmon probably knew hundreds of precedents for *heofonrices weard* and needed only to substitute *heofon* in the alliterating slot.

2a *meotodes meahte*: Repeated verbatim or almost exactly in *And* 694, *Dan* 537, 647, 658, *Gen* 189, *Phx* 6, and *XSt* 164, 352. Lines such as *Dan* 169 " þæt he wolde *metodes* mihte gelyfan " may reflect formulaic feeling for the phrase, but at this early stage of our knowledge perhaps we should confine ourselves to half-line boundaries.[32] The system would be established from *SmS* 228 " full dyslice, dryhtnes meahta " and *Dan* 472 " Onhicgað nu halige mihte " as " (*X'*) mea'ht " ; or from *Glc* 1132 " mod ond mægencræft, þe him meotud engla " and *XSt* 696 " þæt ðu gemettes meotod alwihta ", we might produce " meo'tod (*X'*) ". The former seems more likely, since *meotod* in the first stressed position always alliterates, as far as I can tell. But double alliterating stresses always complicate determinations. *Meotod* ' measurer ' could have referred to Odin, especially in view of its frequent link with *wyrd* in Old English poetry. The following selected examples could also reflect earlier secular diction:

1. *And* 162: gestaðelode strangum mihtum
2. *Bwf* 700: selfes mihtum. Soð is gecyþed
3. *Dan* 350: swylc wæs on þam fyre frean mihtum
4. *Exo* 9: soðfæst cyning, mid his sylfes miht
5. *GfM* 23: under anes meaht ealle forlæte
6. *Whl* 33: þurh dyrne meaht duguðe beswicað.

The verse *dryhtnes meaht-*, where *dryhtnes* could refer to God or earthly rulers, occurs at least eight times in the corpus.[33]

2b *and his modgeþanc*: This phrase occurs exactly in *MBo* 31.19, and close in *MBo* 5.23 " and ðin modgeþonc miclum gedrefan " and *Ele* 535 " ond modgeþanc minne cunnon ". *Modgeþanc-* alone occupies a whole verse in *Dan* 137, *Gen* 93, 1524, 2341, 2647, and *Mxm* I.123. Now one word, no matter how complicated a compound, should probably not be classed as a formula, even if it meets all the metrical requirements of a verse ; it remains just a word (but see below, discussion of 7a). Such compounds broken into elements usually yield systems. One variety parallels other compounds:

1. *Chr* 1315: eagum unclæne ingeþoncas
2. *Dan* 399: breostgeðancum! We þec bletsiað.

This system could be written:

$$\left.\begin{array}{l} \text{mo'd-} \\ \text{breo'st-} \\ \text{in'ge-} \end{array}\right\} \text{geþa''nc-}$$

or " (*X'*)-þa''nc ", or even " (*mi'nd*)-þa''nc ". Separate words may character-

---

[32] Cp. *Bwf* 670, *Dan* 14, *Phx* 471.

[33] *Bwf* 940, *FtA* 56, *Gen* 218, *MBo* 29.35, *Phx* 499, *SmS* 228, *XSt* 230, 604, and perhaps reflected in *Glc* 240 and *SmS* 329.

ize the parallels:

1. *Gen* 631: þurh þæs wraðan geþanc   weorðan sceolden
2. *Jul* 405: in breostsefan   bitre geþoncas
3. *Ps* 50.89: in me, mehtig god,   modswiðne geðanc.

The system is " $(X')$ geþa"nc ".

3a *weorc wuldorfæder*: This verse occurs nowhere else in the corpus ; the compound *wuldorfæder* appears only in *Chr* 217 " worulde þrymmum   mid þinne wuldorfæder " and *Mnl* 147 " mid wuldorfæder   weorca to leane ". These two verses have a different stress pattern from 3a and do not identify the system, also complicated by double alliteration. *Weorc* in the first stressed position of a half-line always alliterates, making it a less likely candidate for the constant element.[34] As with 2b, we might break down the compound to find the system:

1. *Chr* 110: sunu soþan fæder,   swegles in wuldre
2. *XSt* 654: and herigað hehfæder   halgum stefnum
3. *Bwf* 1164: sæton suhterfæderan ;   þa gyt wæs hiera sib ætgædere.

The first two examples could imply the system " $(X')$ $(X')$ fæ"der ", but that produces an unstressed constant. A. J. Bliss labels the third example hypermetric.[35] At this point in my study, I found myself stuck, so I reviewed all the single-line collocations of *weorc* and *wuldor*:

1. *Chr* 1587: ond his weorces wlite   ond wuldres lean
2. *LPr* I.2: geweorðad wuldres dreame.   Sy þinum weorcum halgad
3. *Phx* 386: wunian in wuldre   weorca to leane
4. *Phx* 475: in wuldres byrig   weorca to leane
5. *Phx* 598: wlitige in wuldre.   Weorc anra gehwæs
6. *Chr* 1079: wuldorlean weorca.   Wel is þam þe motun
7. *Glc* 1373: weorca wuldorlean,   willum neotan,

and *Mnl* 147 above. Examples 1-5 tell us only that *weorc* and *wuldre* alliterate, although we might suspect a traditional collocation of the two words. But examples 6 and 7 show another formulaic pattern, reversal of stressed elements, as in *Bwf* 2266 " fela feorhcynna " and *Mxm* I.14 " Feorhcynna fela " (OEFS, 202). *Chr* 1079 and *Glc* 1373 represent essentially the same formula, and imply for verse 3a the system " $(X')$ wu'ldor ".[36] This analysis shows how fluid systematic generation of formulas can be. Since we seek possible patterns in the poet's mind as he composes, we might identify the following from the parallels to 3a:

$(X')$ wu'ldor
we'orc $(X')$

[34] But sometimes the constant can supply the alliteration ; cf. OEFS 202.

[35] A. Bliss, *The Metre of Beowulf* (Oxford: Blackwell, 1962), pp. 88-97, 147.

[36] Textual variations may provide another source of parallels, since in some cases they might represent recomposition or memory errors from formulaic confusion ; cp. the following variants from Dobbie, 22-33:

| O: | wera wuldorfæder | swa he wundra gehwæs |
| Ca: | wera wuldorfæder | swa he wuldres gehwæs |
| $B_1$: | weorc wuldorgodes | swa he wundra fela |
| C: | weoroda wuldorfæder | swa he wundra gehwæs. |

we'orc- wu'ldor-($X''$)

($X'$) ($X'$) fæ''der

*weorc* collocated with *wuldor*.

3b *swa he wundra gehwæs*: Magoun gives as supporting evidence: " **3b** Cp. *frequent* wundra (þæs) fela (*or* worn) *in Grein-Köhler* " (Caedman, 62). No direct repetition of the verse exists, but the following imply a system " (*genitive plural X'*) gehwæ's ":

1. *Bwf* 2397: Swa he niða gehwane   genesen hæfde
2. *Ele* 569: ac hio worda gehwæs   wiðersæc fremedon
3. *Gen* 641: þegnas þolian ;   ac he þeoda gehwam
4. *Phx* 598: wlitige in wuldre.   Weorc anra gehwæs
5. *Run* 84: (Yr) byþ æþelinga   and eorla gehwæs
6. *M Bo* 7.23: sigan sond æfter rene.   Swa bioð anra gehwæs.

(I add this last example to show the problems hypermetric verses cause.) This system " (*gen. pl. X'*) gehwæ's " occurs frequently ; cp. *And* 630, *Bwf* 2838, *Chr* 47, *etc.*, for at least 78 examples.

4a *ece drihten*: This verse appears with various inflections at least 42 times in the corpus, *e.g.*:

1. *Aza* 128: þæt ær gesceop   ece dryhten
2. *Gen* 112: Her ærest gesceop   ece dryhten, *etc.*

Many parallels establish the system " ($X'$) dry'hten ":

1. *Brb* 1: Her Æþelstan cyning,   eorla dryhten
2. *Bwf* 2560: wið ðam gryregieste,   Geata dryhten
3. *Chr* 782: duguða dryhten.   Is þam dome neah
4. *Ele* 346: sigora dryhten.   He on gesyhðe wæs.

This system, as noted above (p. 48), probably originated in pre-Christian and pre-Caedmonian epithets for princes, perhaps even for gods ; *sigora dryhten* would apply to Odin, cp. his names *Sigfaðir* " victory-father " and *Sigrhǫfundr* " victory-judge ".[37]

4b *or onstealde*: This verse occurs in several forms: as written here, *ord astealde, or astelidœ, oord onstealde, etc.*, all essentially meaning the same.[38] It occurs three times elsewhere:

1. *Bwf* 2407: se ðæs orleges   or onstealde
2. *Rdl* 3.59: Ic þæs orleges   or anstelle,
3. *XSt* 113: þe ðes oferhydes   ord onstaldon,

although in each case the poet may deliberately attempt to evoke the memory of *Caedmon's Hymn*, setting the Creation against disaster.[39] *Or/ord* in the

[37] E. O. G. Turville-Petre, *Myth and Religion of the North* (New York: Holt, Rinehart, and Winston, 1964), pp. 50-55 and chap. X. *Sigedryhten* is very common: *And* 60, 877, *Bwf* 391, *Gen* 523, 778, *Glc* 1238, 1375, *Wds* 104, *etc.*

[38] Dobbie, 11-48 ; Frampton, 2 ff. ; and Caedman, 54. Manuscript W has 4b " word astealde ", which Dobbie, 35 ascribes to scribal blunder ; perhaps the scribe could not resist punning on John I.1: " In principio erat Verbum ". Cp. *Bwf* 2791b oð þœt wordes ord.

[39] M. Eliade, *The Myth of the Eternal Return*, trans. W. Trask (Princeton Univ. Press, 2nd corr. printing, 1965), especially chap. 3.

first stressed position, whether in *a*- or *b*-verses, always alliterates (*e.g.*, *Bwf* 1041, *Gen* 6, *Mld* 157, *etc.*). These examples imply the system " ($X'$) onste'llan ":

1. *And* 971: þurh bliðne hige    bysne onstellan
2. *Gen* 911: wrohte onstealdest,    þe þæt wif feoð
3. *Gen* 932: wrohte onstealdest ;    forþon þu winnan scealt
4. *Phx* 511: þonne anwald eal    up astelleð.

5a *He ærest sceop*: This verse appears three more times:

1. *Aza* 128: þæt ær gesceop    ece dryhten
2. *Gen* 112: Her ærest gesceop    ece drihten
3. *MBo* 20.53: ealla gesceafta    ærest gesceope.

The first two may simply copy Caedmon, in view of the *b*-verses. The following establish the system " ($X'$) scie'ppan ":

1. *Aza* 120: Forðon waldend scop    wudige moras
2. *Bwf* 97: leomum ond leafum,    lif eac gesceop
3. *Gen* 308: þa englas of heofnum on helle,    and heo ealle forsceop
4. *Gen* 903: þa nædran sceop    nergend usser
5. *Gen* 1278: æðelinga ord,    þa he Adam sceop[40]
6. *SmS* 373: hu him weorðe geond worold    widsið sceapen.

5b *ielda bearnum*: This verse occurs exactly four times:

1. *Chr* 936: ofer ærworuld    ælda bearnum
2. *Gen* 2472: ungifre yfel    ylda bearnum
3. *Pra* 48: eallum to are    ylda bearnum
4. *Run* 77: (Ac) byþ on eorþan    elda bearnum,

and close three times more:

1. *Bwf* 70: þonne yldo bearn    æfre gefrunon
2. *Bwf* 605: ofer ylda bearn    oþres dogores
3. *OrW* 99: æghwylc ælda bearna    forlæte idle lustas.[41]

The following examples imply the system " ($X'$) bea'rn-":

1. *Bwf* 499: Unferð maþelode,    Ecglafes bearn[42]
2. *Bwf* 888: æþelinges bearn,    ana geneðde
3. *Wld* 2.9: Welandes bearn,    Widia ut forlet
4. *Bwf* 878: þær þe gumena bearn    gearwe ne wiston
5. *Bwf* 1189: Hreðric ond Hroðmund,    ond hæleþa bearn
6. *Gen.* 1554: eall þes middangeard    monna bearnum.

The first three illustrate the secular usefulness of this system as a patronymic. The last three could imply a system " (*Peo'ple*) bea'rn ".[43] Seven manu-

---

[40] Manuscript Ld₁ has 5a *þa he ærest sceop* (Dobbie, 40).

[41] Dobbie, 48 n. 69 cites Old Norse *Völuspá* 20.6 *alda börnum* and Old Saxon *Heliand* 762 *eldeo barn* and 1068C *eldiu barn*. See R. L. Kellogg, " The South Germanic Oral Tradition," in J. B. Bessinger and R. P. Creed, eds., *Franciplegius* (New York Univ. Press, 1965), 66-74.

[42] As noted above, this system can reverse ; cp. *Bwf* 631 " Beowulf maþelode, bearn Ecgþeowes ", reversed for alliterative reasons.

[43] Cp. *Bwf* 1005, 1088, 1141, 2184, *Dan* 73, etc., a very common system.

scripts give verse 5b as *eorðan bearnum*.[44] Dobbie argues convincingly that " *ælda barnum*, as found in the original of M and L and in the *hominum* of the Latin text of Bede, were the words written [*sic*] by Caedmon himself ".[45] We may accept *eorðan bearnum*, nevertheless, as a legitimate reading in a period when textual purity and literary property received scant attention. However, the phrase does not appear outside the variants of *Caedmon's Hymn*, except possibly as reflected in *Sfr* 93 " æþelinga *bearn eorþan* forgiefene ".[46] *Eorðan bearnum* originates from the same system, " (*X'*) bea'rn- ".

6a *heofon to hrofe*: Magoun found no parallels for this verse (Caedman, 54, 63). It has the usual difficulties associated with double alliteration, but simplified by the fact that *heofon* in the first stressed position, whether of *a*- or *b*-verses, always alliterates.[47] The following parallels establish the system " (*X'*) hro'f ":

1. *Bwf* 836: Grendles grape)  under geapne hr[of]
2. *Bwf* 2755: brogdne beadusercean  under beorges hrof
3. *Exo* 298: wrætlicu wægfaru,  oð wolcna hrof
4. *Rdl* 29.7: Ða cwom wundorlicu wiht  ofer wealles hrof
5. *Ruin* 31: hrostbeages [h]rof.  Hryre wong gecrong, *etc*.[48]

Even if none of these sixteen parallels existed, we could establish the system indirectly by these three:

1. *Bwf* 3123: eode eahta sum  under inwithrof
2. *Phx* 173: under heofunhrofe,  þone hatað men
3. *Rdl* 1.10: holme gehrefed,  heahum meahtum.

Examples 1 and 2 yield the system " (*X'*) hro'f " by analyzing compounds. Example 3 has *gehrefed* from the same root as *hrof* and could imply the same system, but perhaps caution should prevent using such peripheral evidence except in desperate cases.

6b *halig scyppend*: Magoun regards 6b as unparallelled (p. 54), but offers this supporting evidence: " Cp. Grein-Köhler for frequent hāliȝ Dryhten and *Chr* 417 milde Sceppend " (Caedman, 63) ; I have never understood why Magoun did not regard *milde Sceppend* as a parallel for *halig Scyppend*. In addition to it, numerous examples establish the system as " (*X'*) scy'ppend ":

1. *Chr* 48: ðara þe geneahhe  noman scyppendes
2. *Chr* 266: ond þin hondgeweorc,  hæleþa scyppend
3. *Dan* 391: and þec Israela,  æhta scyppend
4. *DHl* 109: þæt þu us gemiltsie,  monna scyppend
5. *Ele* 790: þæt me þæt goldhord,  gasta scyppend

---

[44] Manuscripts B₁, Ca, Di, Ld₁, O, P₁, and Tr.

[45] Dobbie, 46-48 ; Frampton ; and 3*NP*, 1-4.

[46] Curiously, *ælda* and *eorðan* tend to collocate: *Chr* 406, 780, *Exo* 437, *Glc* 755, and *Run* 77.

[47] Two possible exceptions: *Ele* 752 heofon ond eorðe ond eall heahmægen, *and Rdl* 87.5 heofones toþe [missing].

[48] Other examples: *Chr* 14, 60, *Dan* 238, 406, 441, *Gen* 153, 956, *Glc* 1313, *MBo* 24.3, *PPs* 54.9.1, and perhaps *Bwf* 403a.

6. *Rdl* 40.1: Ece is se scyppend,   se þas eorþan nu

7. *XSt* 562: Astah up on heofonum   engla scyppend, *etc.*[49]

Even if these thirty parallels had not survived, we might attempt to establish the system indirectly from *Caedmon's Hymn* 5a, *he ærest scop*, again on the principle of common roots in the constants. This system and that of 5a may have originated in pre-Caedmonian diction used for pagan creation scenes, or in secular expressions such as *Bwf* 78b *scop him Heort naman.*

7a *þa middangeard*: This phrase has no exact repetitions in the corpus, but at least 71 instances where *middangeard* alone carries both stresses of a verse, e.g.:

1. *And* 161: þa wæs gemyndig,   se ðe middangeard
2. *Bwf* 75: manigre mægþe   geond þisne middangeard
3. *Gen* 986: þæs middangeard,   monnes swate
4. *Rdl* 66.9: ealne middangeard   ond merestreamas
5. *Rdl* 83.11: middangeardes   mægen unlytel

As with 2b *and his modgeþanc*, we can derive it from a system:

1. *Chr* 55: in þam eardgearde   eawed weorþeð
2. *Chr* 399: flihte lacan   friðgeardum in
3. *Glc* 791: in ecne geard   up gestigan
4. *MBo* 19.9: ne on wingeardum   wlitige gimmas
5. *Phx* 578: fugel on fotum   to frean geardum
6. *SmS* 417: fyr on his frumsceaft   on fæder geardas
7. *SmS* 470: wæter in sende   and wyrmgeardas.

The system should be " ($X'$) gea'rd-". However, I suspect that poets thought of *middangeard* as requiring only one more unstressed word or an inflection to make it a satisfactory verse. Unlike *modgeþanc*, *middangeard* is a very common word (14 versus 78 appearances in poetry). It dates back at least as far in Germanic as Bishop Ulfilas (*ca.* 311-381), who translates οἰκουμένη " the inhabited world " in Luke 2.1, 4.5, and Romans 10.18 as *midjungards* ; it probably originated as a formula in Northern pagan oral literature even before that.[50] The notion of a single word formula causes problems, but in this particular case the designation fits the historical evidence.

7b *moncynnes weard*: This phrase appears two more times in the corpus:

1. *Gen* 2758: milde on mode,   moncynnes weard
2. *Gen* 2896: moncynnes weard,   swa him gemet þinceð.

Its system, " ($X'$) wea'rd ", can be analyzed from the data used for 1b *heofonrices weard*, although either verse could imply a system for the other without further parallels. This phrase could easily describe pre-Caedmonian kings or gods.[51]

---

[49] See also *And* 119, 192, 278, 396, 486, *Chr* 901, 1226, 1395, 1617, *Crd* 21, *Dan* 291, 314, *Gen* 2740, *Glc* 1158, *KtH* 34, *MBo* 29.80, *Pra* 6, 43, *Ps* 50.8, 50.39, *XSt* 242.

[50] J. Grimm, *Teutonic Mythology*, trans. J. S. Stallybrass (London: Bell, 1883 ; repr. New York: Dover, 1966), II, 794. See Kellogg.

[51] The verse *middangeardes weard* appears in *And* 82a, 227a, and *Dan* 596a, perhaps as a product of the " ($X'$) wea'rd " system or a remembrance of line 7a as a whole.

8a *ece drihten*: see 4a above.

8b *æfter teode*: This verse is unique in the corpus. Magoun gives seven parallels, all *æfter* plus a verb, but the following establish the system " (X') teo'n ":

1. *Bwf* 1036: fætedhleore   on flet teon
2. *Bwf* 1332: atol æse wlanc   eftsiðas teah
3. *Bwf* 1439: niða genæged,   ond on næs togen
4. *Rdl* 22.13: swa hine oxa ne teah   ne esna mægen
5. *Rdl* 34.4: hiþeð holdlice   ond to ham tyhð
6. *Rdl* 62.6: hæleð mid hrægle ;   hwilum ut tyhð.[52]

9a *firum foldan*: Magoun found no parallels for this verse (Caedman, 54, 63), and *Exo* 396 " fira æfter foldan,   folmum geworhte " is the closest I find, essentially the same formula.[53] Again, double alliteration complicates analysis. *Fir-* in the first stressed position always alliterates (but then so does *fold-*). The following imply the system " (X') fo'ld- ":

1. *Chr* 279: hatað ond secgað,   hæleð geond foldan
2. *Chr* 1142: muras and stanas   monge æfter foldan
3. *Chr* 1449: dreor to foldan,   þæt þu of deofles þurh þæt
4. *Gen* 1561: geartorhte gife,   grene folde
5. *Gen* 1752: brade foldan.   þu gebletsad scealt
6. *Gen* 2553: sidre foldan   geondsended wæs
7. *Phx* 60: þær ne hægl ne hrim   hreosað to foldan
8. *PPs* 142.4.3: swa þu worulddeade   wrige mid foldan.[54]

9b *frea ælmihtig*: This common epithet appears 18 times. The following establish the system " (X') æ'lmi″htig ":

1. *Chr* 215: ealra cyninga cyning,   Crist ælmihtig
2. *MBo* 20.227: ginfæsta gifa,   god ælmihtig
3. *Gen* 1779: Him þa feran gewat   fæder ælmihtiges
4. *And* 902: Weorð me nu milde,   meotud ælmihtig
5. *Ele* 145: Constantino   cyning ælmihtig
6. *Gen* 2711: hwæðer on þyssum folce   frean ælmihtiges
7. *PPs* 93.20.4: drihten eallmihtig,   dema soðfæst.

Example one is clearly Christian, but 2-4 could imply pre-Caedmonian formulas for pagan gods. 6-7 could describe secular kings, as indeed 5 does.

Now we should have a try at verse 1a, with our principles thus established. Thirteen of the seventeen manuscripts have " Nu *we* sculon herian " in one spelling or another, but the original probably omitted the pronoun (Dobbie,

---

[52] See also *And* 1230, *Bwf* 553, 1051, 1288, *Glc* 144, 354, 649, *Jul* 421, 534, *OrW* 53, and *Rdl* 72.6(?).

[53] Whole-line collocations of *fir-* and *fold-* occur also in *Phx* 3, *Rdl* 33.12, *SmS* 217, 274, 477.

[54] These parallels alliterate on *f*: *And* 918, 1427, 1524, *Bwf* 1196, 2975, *Chr* 807, 983, 1033, 1142, *Dan* 497, *DrR* 132, *Ele* 973, 986, *Exo* 537, *Gen* 154, 1087, 1658, *GfM* 1, *Glc* 396, 808, *Jud* 281, *Jul* 417, *Mnl* 143, *Phx* 74, *Rdl* 7.9, *Run* 88, *SlB* 142, *SmS* 69, 274, 298, 477, *XSt* 263, 493, 531, 544.

11-48). Neither phrase appears in other Old English poetry.[55] As discussed above, Magoun cites four verses:

1. *Gen* 816: Nu me mæg hreowan    þæt ic bæd heofnes god
2. *And* 1517: Nu ðu miht gecnawan    þæt þe cyning engla
3. *Ele* 511: Nu ðu meaht gehyran,    hæleð min se leofa
4. *Bwf* 395: Nu ge moton gangan    in eowrum guðgeatwum.[56]

Following our usual practice of studying only the stresses, we should derive the pattern of " Nu' . . . he'rian " from Magoun's examples as the system " nu' (X') ", perfectly legitimate. But that system gives Caedmon a lot of filling to do ; a one-syllable stressed adverb just is not all that helpful. Perhaps we should attach the unstressed auxiliary verb to *nu* and analyze these parallels:

1. *Chr.* 1327: Nu se sceolon georne    gleawlice þurhseon
2. *Gen* 2276: tregan and teonan.    Nu sceal tearighleor
3. *Gen* 556: on þysne sið sendeð.    Nu sceal he sylf faran
4. *Chr* 15: leomo læmena ;    nu sceal liffrea
5. *Wld* 1.29: beaga mænigo,    nu sceal bega leas
6. *And* 614: forleolc ond forlærde.    Nu hie lungre sceolon
7. *Bwf* 251: ænlic ansyn.    Nu ic eower sceal
8. *And* 66: georn on mode ;    nu ðurh geohða sceal
9. *Chr* 166: nu þu freode scealt    fæste gedælan
10. *HbM* 9: on ceolþele,    ond nu cunnan scealt
11. *Glc* 582: halig in heortan.    Nu þu in helle scealt
12. *Glc* 670: engla gemana.    Swa nu awa sceal
13. *Rsg* 42: of þisse worulde,    nu ic wat þæt ic sceal.

The system might be " nu' sculan (X') ", and the examples above, every collocation in one verse of *nu* and *sculan* I found, show it to be reasonably common. Examples 6-13 might imply a certain fluidity in placing the alliterating element or imply the system " nu' (X') sculan ".[57] Although I find these two systems possible, I prefer to remain conservatively restricted to stressed positions so early in our knowledge of formulaic patterning. So I wish to propose the system " (X') he'rian " on the basis of the following 44 parallels:

1. *Bwf* 1833: wordum ond worcum,    þæt ic þe wel herige
2. *Bwf* 3175: þæt mon his winedryhten    wordum herge
3. *Exo* 547: dugoð on dreame    drihten herigað
4. *XSt* 659: Swa wuldres weard    wordum herigað, *etc.*[58]

[55] " We sculon God herian " opens each office in a tenth century Benedictine liturgy ; see 3*NP*, 38 n. 1. This may reflect Caedmon's influence or perhaps his source, since he may have heard similar offices if they were performed at Whitby in the seventh century.

[56] Caedmon, 62. Magoun quotes only half-lines, a mistake in my opinion ; having the whole line in mind increases our understanding of the intricacies and deceptiveness of stress patterns and inter-verse relations. Besides, the poet composed that way.

[57] Manuscript B$_1$ reads " Nu we herigan sculon " (Dobbie, 28).

[58] See also *And* 657, 722, 1267, 1455, *Aza* 3, 68, 94, 118, 146, 154, *Chr* 470, 503, *Crd* 50, *Dan* 256, 281, 357, 374, 421, *Ele* 892, 1096, 1220, *Exo* 576, *Gen* 2, 15, 1855, *Jul* 60, *LPr* 2.122, 2.24, *MBo* 10.26, 30.6, *PPs* 55.4.1, 55.9.1., 62.4.3, 65.1.2, 70.7.4, 73.19.3, 116.1.3, 118.175.1, *SmS* 24, and perhaps *Mxm* 1.4.

However, in 1a, *herian* alliterates, seemingly violating the pattern. But, in many cases, the constant will alliterate, freeing the poet from seeking an alliterating element, as in these examples:[59]

1. *Aza* 135: heanne hergen. Ful oft þu hluttor lætest
2. *Dan* 386: Hwalas ðec herigað, and hefonfugolas
3. *Dan* 404: We ðec herigað, halig drihten
4. *GfM* 93: hlude hergan, hafað healice
5. *Glo* 1.36: Ealle þe heriað halige dreamas
6. *Jul* 77: on hyge hergan, oþþe hi nabban
7. *KtH* 7: We ðe heriað halgum stefnum
8. *Rim* 19: horsce mec heredon, hilde generedon.

The system for 1a is " $(X')$ he'rian ", with the constant *herian* alliterating.

This method of analysis meets my three objections to Magoun's underlining and supporting evidence. First, it accounts for all the verses, not just Magoun's " eighty-three-plus percent of the language of the *Hymn* " (Caedman, 54 ; a dubiously high percentage using Magoun's methods), and without the need for a larger surviving corpus. A. H. Smith says that " nine or more of its eighteen half-lines can be parallelled in other poems " (3*NP*, 15, and n. 1), but this mode parallels every line. Second, it alleviates *some* of the mechanical side of Magoun's presentation. I admit it remains somewhat mechanical itself, as must any analysis which spells out the steps. (Try breaking down any simple daily activity without sounding mechanical, *e.g.*, walking). Third, and most important, it shows us the poet at work. If, for example, a poet wanted a one-verse epithet for deity protecting the sky, the pool of systems supplies him this one, " $(X')$ wea'rd ", with this potential:

$$\left. \begin{array}{l} engla \\ upengla \\ heah\ hordes \\ heofonrices \\ rodera \\ heofones \\ swegles \end{array} \right\} \quad weard.$$

He has alliterative possibilities of vowels, *h*, *r*, *s*, and *w*. Of course, alliterative fillers parallelled from the corpus do not exhaust his wordhoard ; we could add, e.g., *wolcna*.[60] This exposition of the method also meets the objections of Ann Watts: " Fry's obliteration of a distinction between formula and formulaic system goes far to describe in a useful way the conventionality of Old English poetic diction ; but it does not describe at all the method of composition of Old English poems or of any poetry that consistently employs

[59] OEFS, 202 ; cp. notes 34 and 54 above. Notice that the constants participate in double alliteration in *Caedmon's Hymn* 2a, 3a, 6a, and 9a.

[60] This type of formulaic potential analysis will be facilitated by a computer-produced English-Old English dictionary now being produced by my graduate assistant Patricia Gardner.

phrases of a highly traditional character ".[61] This mode *does* describe the mode of composition ; for example, it shows how Caedmon might have created 4a and 8a *ece drihten* from epithets for princes:

$$\left.\begin{array}{l} eorla \\ weoruda \\ mihtig \\ dugu\eth a \\ ure, etc. \end{array}\right\} drihten.$$

The process I have described attempts to capture the potential of the generating systems, by setting the half-line the poet actually composed against the system which produced it originally. In fact, the systems would remain only patterns in the poet's mind, probably never reaching the level of self-consciousness required for our critical purposes. If he knew and remembered a pre-existent verse which fitted all his needs, he used it ; if he did not recall such a verse, his pool of systems would produce one for him. Poets compose by " ear " and " feel ", not by rules of metre, alliterative fillers, constants, etc. All this cumbersome paraphernalia attempts to capture for us that " feel " and that " ear ". Poetry runs ; criticism puts the right foot in front of the left, the left foot in front of the right, etc.

One might reasonably object that this method simply describes Old English metre in a different way ; " $(X')$ dri'hten " means no more than that each verse requires two stresses and alliteration. I would turn that around and speculate that Germanic formulas preceded and ultimately produced Germanic metre. The " feel " of a line was four important words stressed, with alliteration linking the hemistichs. Traditional two-stress collocations grew over a period of time, and the poets learned the resultant patterns, patterns of variously repeated verses (i.e., formulas) and patterns of form from the formulas (i.e., systems). Old English metre has very simple requirements, once the poet knows formulaic patterning. Try collocating two important stressed Old English words in a grammatical unit with alliteration rules satisfied and enough particles to yield four to eleven syllables ; the result almost invariably fits one of Sievers's five types.

## III

This analysis is anachronistic, using post-Caedmonian verses to explain Caedmon. But I find it more likely that the half-lines in the corpus originated in systems Caedmon used than that Caedmon originated the systems himself. That would be a miracle. Caedmon did begin Old English Christian vernacular poetry, the value of which Abbess Hild and her scholars immediately recognized. Bede tells us nothing of their motives, only that Hild perceived God's grace and provided Caedmon with leisure and encouragement to turn sacred history and doctrine into verse. Hild's reputation shows

[61] Watts, 69. She misunderstands my notion of systems: " Fry gives *heals-beaga mæst, heall-cerna mæst* and *fela feorhcynna, feorhcynna fela* as examples of formulaic systems " (p. 69). I did not give those two sets of phrases as " examples of formulaic systems ", but as evidence implying the systems.

a clever woman who spent the first half of her life as a princess and the rest as a nun, sharp in her judgments and devoted to the spread of Christianity and learning (*H.E.*, IV, 23). I suspect that Hild grasped the potential of converting the secular poetry of the Germans to Christian uses, in the spirit of Pope Gregory's admonition to Abbot Mellitus to convert pagan temples into churches, because the English " will be able to banish error from their hearts and be more ready to come to the places they are familiar with, but now recognizing and worshipping the true God ".[62] Caedmon did just that.

DONALD K. FRY

*State University of New York*
*Stony Brook*

---

[62] *H.E.*, I, 30 ; Colgrave and Mynors, 107.

# FROM ILLITERACY TO LITERACY: PROLEGOMENA TO A STUDY OF THE *NIBELUNGENLIED*

The application of the theory of Milman Parry and Albert B. Lord to the *Nibelungenlied* has established its oral-formulaic and oral-thematic content.[1] Its provenience in oral tradition must therefore be assumed unless (1) an exclusively written transmission of the epic prior to the late twelfth century can be established in defiance of everything we know of medieval German culture between the time of the origins of the narrative during the period of the migrations and the late twelfth century ; or (2) the determinants of oral transmission in the *Nibelungenlied*—densely formulaic style and thematic composition—can be shown not to be determinants of oral transmission but something else.[2] In this respect two types of argument are to be avoided: (a) the common attempt to negate densely formulaic style as indicator of oral transmission by adducing evidence of formulaic style in written compositions such as Middle Latin riddles, the OE *Phoenix*, or the *Meters of Boethius*, and (b) the attempt to confine the function of formulicity to surface style, to regard it as non-functional in the process of composition, to ascribe it merely to " fashion " or the incapacity of the poet. The first argument presupposes the validity of generalizing the application of the criteria of the Parry-Lord theory from epic narratives, which yielded the criteria, to any other genre. Methodologically the argument is therefore irrelevant.[3] The second argument can carry weight only if it succeeds in

[1] Franz H. Bäuml and Donald J. Ward, " Zur mündlichen Überlieferung des Nibelungenliedes," *DVLG*, 41 (1967), 351-390 ; Franz H. Bäuml, " Der Übergang mündlicher zur Artes-bestimmten Literatur des Mittelalters: Gedanken und Bedenken," *Fachliteratur des Mittelalters. Festschrift für Gerhard Eis* (Stuttgart, 1970), pp. 1-10 ; Franz H. Bäuml and Agnes M. Bruno, " Weiteres zur mündlichen Überlieferung des Nibelungliedes," *DVLG*, 46 (1972), 479-493 ; and Edward Haymes, *Mündliches Epos in mittelhochdeutscher Zeit* (Diss., Erlangen, 1969).

[2] Cf. Bäuml and Bruno, *DVLG*, 46 (1972), 479-493, particularly pp. 480-483, for a more detailed discussion of these points.

[3] Cf., e.g. Jackson. J. Campbell, " Learned Rhetoric in Old English Poetry ", *MP*, 63 (1966), 189-201, and Larry D. Benson, " The Literary Character of Anglo-Saxon Formulaic Poetry ", *PMLA*, 81 (1966), 334-341. The attempt, for instance, to apply the Parry-Lord theory to balladry has failed signally, c.f. James H. Jones, " Commonplace and Memorization in the Oral Tradition of the English and Scottish Popular Ballads ", *JAF*, 74 (1961), 97-112, and Albert Friedman, " The Formulaic-Improvisation Theory of Ballad Tradition—A Counter-Statement ", ibid., pp. 113-115 ; on the other hand, its possible applicability to certain types of sermons must be conceded, cf. Bruce A. Rosenberg, " The Formulaic Quality of Spontaneous Sermons ", *JAF*, 83 (1970), 3-20. It is curious that Claes Schaar's warning (*Neophil.*, 40 [1956], 301-305) directed against hasty application of the Parry-Lord theory, that " oral poetry is formulaic " is not synonymous with " formulaic poetry is oral," was not heeded by critics of the theory. In part it is this misapplication of the criterion of formulaic style as determinant of oral composition, and in part an uncritical use of the concept " oral composition ", which has led to the creation of a quasi-problem: the concept of the transitional text. Already in 1962, Robert D. Stevick, " The Oral-Formulaic Analyses of Old English Verse ", *Speculum*, 37 (1962), 382-389, warned against such misapplications and the use of certain undefined concepts. The very possibility of the existence of a " transitional text " is denied by Lord and insisted upon by those who have found evidence of for-

demonstrating that formulicity fulfils a different function in the *Nibelungen-lied* from that established for oral epic by Parry and Lord. Since it has not been possible to ascribe to the density of formulaic style and thematic composition of the *Nibelungenlied* a function other than that demonstrated for formulicity in epic narrative, it is logical to conclude that its transmitted written texts rest upon prior—and conceivably simultaneous—oral transmission.

This does not mean, however, that the transmitted written versions of the *Nibelungenlied* are records of an oral performance. If this were the case, the density of formulae would be relatively stable throughout the text. But this is not the case: the density of formulaic constructions varies from 25% to 80% per stanza. It is therefore logical to conclude that the oral tradition —probably in the form of a written record of an oral performance—served as the basis for the written composition of the transmitted text by a literate poet for a literate audience.[4] The oral tradition, in short, was adapted to other purposes and other perceptions: an orally transmitted heroic epic was transformed by a learned poet into a courtly epic. It is our purpose in this paper to indicate briefly some implications of this shift from the oral to the literate realms of perception, and thus to lay the foundation for an application of the literary-historical facts of orality and literacy to literary criticism.[5]

Oral poetry is the poetry of the illiterate. The poet composes his narrative by means of traditional themes, and expresses these in traditional,

mulaic composition in works unquestionably composed by a writing poet. The apparent contradiction of these two contentions arises from two different uses of the concept " oral " and " oral composition ": e.g. (1) ". . . we must admit [the possibility of transitional texts] only if it is indeed true that a formulaic writer inevitably composed in the traditional way, with his lines and his poems shaped by the demands of oral composition despite the use of the pen . . ." (Benson, *PMLA*, 81 [1966], 337) ; (2) the question is " whether there can be a single individual who in composing an epic would think now in one way and now in another, or, perhaps, in a manner that is a combination of two techniques. I believe that the answer must be in the negative, because the two techniques are, I submit, contradictory and mutually exclusive " (Lord, *The Singer of Tales* [Cambridge, Mass., 1964], p. 129). It therefore depends on whether emphasis is placed on the *procedure* of composition (pen in hand or not) or on the *means* of composition (formulae or not). If the *procedure* of composition is emphasized, i.e. not " oral " or " written ", but " reciting " or " writing ", then one can clearly speak of transitional texts in characterizing the formulaic products of writing poets, such as the *Phoenix*, the *Meters of Boethius*, or the OS *Heliand*. This now receives support from the findings of Bruce A. Rosenberg, *supra*, pp. 18-20. If, however, the *means* of composition is stressed, i.e. *necessarily* formulaic or *not necessarily* formulaic (Lord, *Singer of Tales*, p. 130), then a " transitional " mode of composition is indeed unthinkable. And the same can be said of the " text ": if the text consists for the most part of formulaic constructions, then it is indebted to the oral tradition, whether it was composed pen in hand or not. Cf. Bäuml in *Fachliteratur des Mittelalters*, pp. 1-10 as well as Bäuml and Bruno, *DVLG*, 46 (1972), 479-493, for more detailed discussion.

[4] Cf. Bäuml and Bruno, *DVLG*, 46 (1972), 479-493, for a brief description of the computer-based analysis of stylistic heterogeneity by Agnes M. Bruno, *Compositional Heterogeneity in the Nibelungenlied: Toward a Quantative Methodology for Stylistic Analyses* (Diss., Univ. of Calif., Los Angeles, 1971).

[5] For an application of the following to a specific problem, cf. Bäuml, " Transformations of the Heroine: From Epic Heard to Epic Read ", to appear in *The Role of the Woman in the Middle Ages*, ed. Rosmarie T. Morewedge (Albany, 1974).

rhythmically organized units, i.e. formulae, defined by Parry as " a group of words which is regularly employed under the same metrical conditions to express a given essential idea ".[6] It is well known that, since both themes and formulae are protean, i.e. adaptable to a given context and not memorized—only a fixed text is memorizable—each performance of a poem will vary from each other performance. As a rule this variation, unless it is marked by crass differences in length, is noticeable only to the literate observer, who perceives a performance as a " text ", as a series of words which he compares to another " text ". Within the oral tradition, however, such concepts as " variant ", " original ", " conflation ", are irrelevant: the illiterate audience does not possess the means to make the comparisons underlying these concepts.[7]

Illiteracy is usually regarded merely as the absence of literacy. This is an oversimplification. There are at least two distinct types of illiteracy: (a) pre-literacy, i.e. the illiteracy of an entire society, and (b) the illiteracy of a subgroup within a literate society.[8] The society of Homeric Greece and the tribal societies of central and northern Europe before and during the period of the migrations are examples of preliterate societies. Writing (Linear B, the runic alphabet) was known, but not used for discursive communication. The transmission of the knowledge necessary for the functioning of a preliterate society, for a consciousness of its very identity —law, myth, rules of conduct, genealogy, etc.—was oral. Oral poetry, therefore, fulfilled an encyclopaedic function, transmitting the very fundament of preliterate society. This function, together with the physical and social determinants of the transmission (recitation, perception) of oral poetry defines its " meaning " in an illiterate or preliterate environment. It will therefore be necessary to cast a brief glance at those determinants before contrasting them with those operative in the social context of literacy.[9]

[6] " Studies in the Epic Technique of Oral Verse-Making I ", *Harvard Studies in Classical Philology*, 41 (1930), 80, and Lord, *Singer of Tales*, p. 30. Underlying these " semantic formulae " are, of course, " syntactic formulae " or " syntactic frames ". Cf. Wayne O'Neil, *Oral-Formulaic Structure in OE Elegiac Poetry* (Diss., Wisconsin, 1960) and particularly Godfrey L. Gattiker, *The Syntactic Basis of the Poetic Formula in Beowulf* (Diss., Wisconsin, 1962) and Donald C. Green, " Formulas and Syntax in OE Poetry ", *Computers and the Humanities*, 6 (1971), 85-93. The proposition of Edward de Chasca in " Toward a Redefinition of Epic Formula in the Light of the *Cantar de Mio Cid* ", *HR*, 38 (1970), 251-263, can be criticized precisely because it does not include a consideration of the implications of a shift from orality to literacy. An approach toward isolation of different strata of formulaic economy to distinguish between dictation and adaptation of an oral text is suggested by William Whallon, " Who Wrote Down the Formulaic Poem? ", *Actes du Vᵉ Congrès de l'Association Internationale de Littérature Comparée* (Amsterdam, 1969), 469-472. That the basis of formulicity is not to be sought in syntactic structure, as for instance by Edward Haymes, is shown by Michael Nagler, " Oral Poetry and the Question of Originality in Literature ", *Actes*, 451-459. Cf. in this regard also the important essay of Nagler, " Towards a Generative View of the Oral Formula ", *TAPA*, 98 (1967), 269-311.

[7] *Singer of Tales*, pp. 22, 26-29, 68-98, 124-138.

[8] J. L. Myres, " Folk Memory ", *Folklore*, 37 (1926), 13-24, and Bäuml, in *The Role of the Woman . . .*, ed. Morewedge.

[9] For the best analysis of the function of oral poetry in a pre-literate society, and the basis for much of the following, cf. Eric A. Havelock, *Preface to Plato* (Cambridge, Mass., 1963), particularly chapters II-V, VII-XIII.

Oral poetry is perceived through the ear. An oral epic therefore has only two modes of existence: it exists in the individual recitation and in memory. Since its subject-matter was vital for the existence of the society it served, its preservation was vital, and since it could only be preserved in memory, all aspects of recitation had to serve memory. No other oral genre can achieve this vital, though flexible link between matter and mnemonic devices ; it is therefore the oral epic which is uniquely suited to perform an encyclopaedic function in preliterate society.[10] The essential retention of the extensive subject-matter of the oral epic is served by four circumstances: (1) the familiarity of traditional narrative themes and their lexical vehicles, the oral formulae, which were also anchored in tradition ;[11] (2) the necessity of presenting all narrative elements of an oral narrative paratactically as actions or occurrences: " Kantian imperatives and mathematical relationships and analytic statements are inexpressible and also unthinkable. . . . all ' knowledge ' in an oral culture is temporally conditioned, . . . " ;[12] (3) the rhythmical organization of oral delivery, which defines the traditional formulae and derives additional mnemonic effectiveness from the fact that " it is easiest to excite [bodily reflexes of larynx or limbs] through words if the words themselves evoke action and hence if they describe action " ;[13] (4) a high degree of visual suggestion, since all narrative elements are stated as actions or occurrences each of which is complete in itself (the function of the oral theme furthers the independence of these elements).[14]

The rhythmical recitation of a chain of easily visualized actions in the form of traditional themes and formulae serves its mnemonic purpose by aiding the identification of the audience with the narrative.[15] The distance between narrative and audience is further reduced by the cultural context of oral epic performance: since the content of the epic fulfils a cultural necessity for preliterate society—and to some degree for an illiterate subgroup of a literate society—and since the compositional and lexical forms (themes and formulae) into which this content is cast are traditional, there is no distinction between poet and " narrator " or poet and text: the poet, representing a cultural tradition, is the " narrator ", and his narration is the tradition in both form and content. This situation is graphically depicted in the first stanza of the *Nibelungenlied*. Initially the poet-reciter-narrator is at one with the audience as recipient of the tradition: " Uns ist in alten maeren wunders vil geseit," and in the last line he separates himself, as vehicle for the transmission of that tradition, from the audience (" ir "): " mugt ir nu wunder hoeren sagen ".

[10] Havelock, pp. 36-86.

[11] Havelock, pp. 88-89, 91-93.

[12] Havelock, pp. 171-174, 180-182, 185-187 ; Howard Becker and Harry E. Barnes, *Social Thought from Lore to Science* (New York, 1961), I, 15-16.

[13] Havelock, pp. 148-154, 166-167.

[14] Havelock, pp. 67-84, 174-179, 187-188.

[15] Havelock, pp. 145-160 ; R. G. Collingwood, *The Principles of Art* (Oxford, 1938), p. 315.

No doubt these characteristics of oral transmission contribute to the homoeostatic character, the cultural amnesia, of preliterate cultures: whatever of the past is not relevant for the present is eliminated or changed to a form which renders it relevant.[16] Oral poetry likewise exhibits no consciousness of the past as past, but constantly adapts its narrative matter to the context of the present.[17] The dense formulicity—and therefore presumably oral origin—of some of the " courtly " passages of the *Nibelungenlied* may serve as illustration of the absorption of contemporary elements into a preexisting context.

The above attributes characterize the oral tradition of a preliterate society as well as that of an illiterate subgroup of a literate society. In the latter, however, some aspects of the function and the situation of oral poetry are different from the function and situation which characterize it in preliterate society. Since, by definition, the knowledge essential to the perpetuation of society—law, religion, etc.—is transmitted in writing in a literate society, illiterate subgroups within such a society also have no need to depend on oral poetry for the transmission of such knowledge. The importance of the encyclopaedic function of such poetry for these subgroups will have been reduced, just as the social importance of the illiterate subgroup within a literate society was reduced. Likewise, the situation of the oral poetry in an illiterate subgroup of a literate society is distinct from that in a preliterate society. The proximity of oral poetry to the literate environment makes it possible to fix it in writing and perceive it through the eye in a literate context.[18] It will therefore be necessary to investigate briefly some implications of such a shift.

A written text exists independently of the reader and his memory. It can be forgotten, gone back to, re-read, or read in different sequences. It will remain the same unless it is changed purposely. The homoeostasis occasioned by oral transmission is therefore absent in written transmission.[19] The written text also exists independently of the poet: once it is written down and no longer in his hands, the poet ceases to exercise control over it, and its effect does not depend on his presence. It is therefore obvious to

[16] Rüdiger Schott, " Das Geschichtsbewusstsein schriftloser Völker ", *Archiv für Begriffsgeschichte*, 12 (1968), 184, 197 ; Maurice Halbwachs, *Les cadres sociaux de la mémoire* (Paris, 1925) ; " Mémoire et société ", *L'Année sociologique*, 1 (1940-48), 11-177 ; *La Mémoire collective* (Paris, 1950) ; and Frederic C. Bartlett, *Psychology and Primitive Culture* (Cambridge, 1923), pp. 42-43, 62-63, 256.

[17] Jack Goody and Ian Watt, " The Consequences of Literacy ", *Comparative Studies in Society and History*, 5 (1963), 304-45, particularly 307-311. Oswald Spengler's formulation in *Der Untergang des Abendlandes* (München, 1924), II, 180, is particularly succinct: " Die Schrift ist eine ganz neue Sprachart und bedeutet eine völlige Abänderung der menschlichen Wachseinsbeziehungen, indem sie sie vom Zwange der Gegenwart befreit ".

[18] These points are considered in more detail in Bäuml, " Transformations of the Heroine: . . .", *The Role of the Woman* . . ., ed. Morewedge.

[19] The remarkable stability of vocabulary within literacy is illustrated by Marjorie S. Zengel, " Literacy as a Factor in Language Change ", *AA*, 64 (1962), 132-139 and in *Readings in the Sociology of Language*, ed. J. A. Fishman (The Hague and Paris, 1968), pp. 296-304.

the listener to a recitation of a written text that the reciter is not the poet. In addition, the " narrator " becomes distinct from the poet as well as from the text, upon which he can now comment.[20] One of many examples of such commentary by the fictional " narrator " upon the text of the *Nibelungenlied* occurs in st. 680, 1.2: " Dar zuo nam er ir gürtel, daz was ein porte guot./ Ine weiz ob er daz taete durh sînen hôhen muot ". It is clear that the source of the commentary, the poet, casts the " narrator " in the role of commentator upon the text and thereby places distance between himself and the " narrator ", between the " narrator " and the text, as well as between the reciter and the text, since the reciter is now also free to comment upon the text by inflection and gesture. In short, both the poet, by means of his " narration ", and the reciter can confront the text, i.e. the tradition—a stance impossible for the oral poet-reciter-narrator: the literate poet, as well as the reciter, can take issue with the text, and as far as the narrative matter of the text is traditional, they can challenge the tradition which—unlike the oral poet—they no longer embody and represent.

This increase in distance between the various aspects of literary narration —poet, " narrator ", reciter, text, perceiver—now gives full scope to the functions of irony. The perception of irony depends on double participation: one participator in an ironic situation participates or perceives without understanding, the other participates or perceives with an understanding of the situation as well as of the lack of understanding of the other participator. Numerous passages of the *Nibelungenlied* have been identified as ironical, but these identifications disregard the fact that the perception of at least certain types of irony hinges upon literacy and that it therefore signals a " new " understanding of the *Nibelungenlied* around 1200—that it is part of the shift in the " meaning " of the poem occasioned by its crossing the line from illiterate (unstable aural) to literate (visual or stable aural) perception.[21] Literacy in this context has little to do with the literacy of individuals. It is immaterial that the majority of the population of thirteenth century Germany—of any social class but the clerical—was illiterate.[22] Literate

[20] For some further implications of the development of the " narrator " in fiction, cf. Robert Scholes and Robert Kellogg, *The Nature of Narrative* (New York, 1966), pp. 55-56 ; also Hansjürgen Linke, " Über den Erzähler im Nibelungenlied und seine künstlerische Funktion ", *GRM*, 41 (1960), 370-385.

[21] Cf., for instance, the following on irony in the *Nibelungenlied*: Hugh Sacker, " On Irony and Symbolism in the *Nibelungenlied*: Two Preliminary Notes ", *GLL*, 14 (1960-61), 271-281, particularly pp. 271-276 ; D. G. Mowatt and H. Sacker, *The Nibelungenlied: An Interpretative Commentary* (Toronto, 1967) ; Hugo Bekker, *The Nibelungenlied: A Literary Analysis* (Toronto and Buffalo, 1971). For a typology of irony, cf. D. H. Green, " Irony in Medieval Romance ", *FMLS*, 5 (1970), 49-64.

[22] It should be kept in mind, however, that in the thirteenth century literacy appears to have increased rapidly among the laity in Germany ; cf. James Westfall Thompson, *The Literacy of the Laity in the Middle Ages* (New York, 1963), pp. 82-115, and the literature cited in Karl Hauck, " Haus- und sippengebundene Literatur mittelalterlicher Adelsgeschlechter ", *Geschichtsdenken und Geschichtsbild im Mittelalter*, ed. W. Lammers [Wege der Forschung, 21] (Darmstadt, 1961), p. 166, n. 4. On the irrelevance of individual literacy for the " literate " orientation of illiterate reciters, cf. Lord, *The Singer of Tales*, pp. 137-138.

perception is dependent not on the individual's ability to read and write, but on his perceptual orientation within his literate culture: the recognition of the fact that the fundaments of his culture—codified laws, the doctrine of the Church—are transmitted in writing, and his consequent reliance, if not on his own literacy, then on that of others for the acquisition of knowledge. Knowledge thus acquired will be perceived as existing independently of the process of acquisition (reading) and as stable: each time the source is consulted, it will yield the same data.

The literate audience of the *Nibelungenlied*,—i.e. the reader, or the audience of a reading or a memorized recitation of the *Nibelungenlied*—is able to look back upon the narrative. This is the result, not of individual literacy, but of exposure to noticeably inert texts. The limited number of textual traditions represented by the thirty-four transmitted manuscripts testifies to the stability of the written tradition. The reader or audience of this written tradition can therefore be assumed to know this inert narrative from other readings or memorized recitations. The illiterate listener to an oral performance has neither a stable textual basis as a point of reference, nor a stable textual tradition as a point of textual comparison.[23] The reader or literate audience, moreover, is able to perceive the basis of textual stability: words as semantic forms. The illiterate listener receives the semantic " message " of an epic not through the perception of words, but of traditional formulae. Formulae such as " ein degen küen unde balt ", " ein sneller degen guot ", etc. function as traditional epic epithets. Just as the formula is the *necessary* tool of composition for the oral poet, it also forms the basis of semantic perception for the listener.[24] To the writing poet and the literate audience any given word is not in itself necessary within its context in the same sense as a formula is necessary within the traditional context which it transmits. A word or series of words can be isolated from a context, since a word is not dependent on its context, nor is it perceived in terms of a tradition.[25] The formula, on the other hand, is dependent on its context: it is suggested by the narrative theme, both to the poet and the listener. In short, the distance is not only greater between literate poet and written text than between oral poet and recitation, it is also greater between written text and literate perceiver than between recitation and illiterate listener. The literate perceiver can isolate the word from the depicted action and confront the word with the action it describes: if the description does not fit the action, irony is the result. In crossing the line into the realm of

[23] For some consequences of textual instability, cf. C. M. Bowra, *Heroic Poetry* (London, 1952), pp. 299-329. The absence of textual stability in oral tradition extends even to singers who have learned to write ; cf. Lord, " The Influence of a Fixed Text ", *To Honor Roman Jakobson* (The Hague and Paris, 1967), II, 1199-1206.

[24] The *necessity* of the formula for oral composition is the crucial distinction between oral and literate composition ; cf. *The Singer of Tales*, p. 130, and Bäuml in *Fachliteratur des Mittelalters*, pp. 1-10 as well as Bäuml and Bruno in *DVLG*, 46 (1972), 483-485.

[25] Bäuml in *The Role of the Woman . . .*, ed. Morewedge, and Lord, *The Singer of Tales*, p. 133.

literacy, the epic epithet became a characterization, which may or may not be ironized by the action of the character to whom it is applied. One of many examples: " sprach daz minneclîche wîp " is a formula, and as such no different from " sprach diu minneclîche meit " or a dozen others. But a literate audience perceives words, not formulae, as semantic units. The last half-line of st. 425—

> " Den stein sol er werfen    unt springen darnâch,
> den gêr mit mir schiezen.    lât iu sîn niht ze gâch.
> ir muget wol hie verliesen    die êre und ouch den lîp.
> des bedenket iuch vil ebene ",    sprach daz minneclîche wîp.

—an oral epic formula, can be perceived by a literate audience as ironic: " minneclîche " can be separated from its traditional formulaic context and, as separate semantic unit, it no longer simply denotes the speaker, but characterizes her. This characterization, in light of her preceding proclamation, is clearly ironic.

Just as the " meaning " of a formula, an epic epithet, can change in crossing the boundary between illiteracy and literacy without lexical alteration, the ahistorically paratactic elements of the oral epic, the result—and possibly one of the causes—of the homoeostasis of illiterate society, are likely to be perceived as symbolic by literate society. Homoeostasis, the incapacity of illiterate cultures to conceive of the past as past, is of course due, in part, to the nature of the oral transmission of the past. The fact that the process of transmission, of preservation of the past, must constantly be repeated within a context which is no longer that of the past being transmitted, ensures the constant adaptation of the transmitted past to the demands of the present.[26] The inevitable result is a paratactic arrangement of chronologically or causally irreconcilable episodes reflecting different cultural strata: e.g. the mention of the two youths of Siegfried, the heroic and the courtly ; the entire Isenstein episode, etc. Within the context of literacy, however, the record of the past is stable since it is not dependent for its very existence on its recitation and repetition in the present: it is recorded in writing and—except for acts of destruction of the material object on which it is recorded—will be preserved whether it is noticed or not. As a preserved record it is therefore not adapted to reflect the present and it does not support a homoeostatic view of the past. It can be interpreted, to be sure, but it cannot itself identify the past with the present. The literate perceiver, therefore, in being confronted by a homoeostatic depiction of events, may be conscious of inconsistencies which cannot be perceived by the illiterate listener. This is amply demonstrated by Nibelungen-scholarship, which since its inception has emphasized differences in " layers " of narrative which the poet did not unite to the satisfaction of the modern critic. These inconsistencies, however, are resolved by the

[26] Cf. Goody and Watt, " The Consequences of Literacy ", *Comp. Stud. in Society and History*, 5 (1963), 307-311.

medieval reader in terms of his own perception of a written text—a perception formed by his exposure to predominantly elucidative literature.

The encyclopaedic function of oral epic poetry demands that such poetry be essentially representational of the external world and of relationships in that world as they are understood by the culture dependent upon it: it is essentially mimetic.[27] The incongruities in such a representation will, however, be noted by a literate audience, which, as a consequence, will no longer be able to preceive it as " representational ", as mimetic, but will be led by its own literary experience to perceive it symbolically, or " illustratively." For when an oral poem crosses the line from an illiterate subgroup to a literate society it also crosses from one social level to another. In the case of the *Nibelungenlied*, it entered the socially privileged (literate) stratum of society to which the works of Hartmann, Wolfram, and Gottfried were addressed. This audience will therefore bring to the written *Nibelungenlied* the same tools of perception which it applies to other stable texts, and which can only be applied to such texts: it will perceive the *Nibelungenlied* not as " representing " a chain of exemplary actions, but as " illustrating " a series of problems. In crossing the line from illiteracy to literacy, from a disadvantaged to a privileged social stratum, the *Nibelungenlied* could not remain what it was in its oral stage, an account of actions, but had to become a commentary upon them. Siegfried's behavior upon his arrival at Worms, or Brünhild's *unmilte* in exclaiming that Gunther's " kameraere mir wil der mînen wât lâzen niht belîben " (517), for instance, will be perceived differently by the two different audiences: the literate audience is in a position to view both passages as ironic, the illiterate audience is not. The latter's homoeostatic view of society prevents it from noting the anachronisms or discrepancies which make possible the perception of these passages as ironic. Furthermore, the very function of the oral epic in an illiterate society prevents an ironic view of the " culture hero ", who, after all, is the principal vehicle for the didactic, exemplary content of the epic.[28] A hero ironized is no longer a hero, for in being ironized he is no longer admired, but judged

[27] Cf. Havelock, pp. 44-45, 145-160.

[28] Cf. Havelock, p. 168: " In sum, the saga, in order to do its job for the community and offer an effective paradigm of social law and custom, must deal with those acts which are conspicuous and political. And the actors who alone can furnish these paradigms in this kind of [preliterate] society we designate as ' heroes.' The reason for the heroic paradigm is in the last resort not functional but technical ". But it is not only this function of the hero which prevents his ironization in oral epic—to some degree, in fact, he has shed a purely " political " function in the context of a disadvantaged illiterate subgroup within a literate society, since such a subgroup has no use for the lessons to be learned from such a function. To whatever degree the hero retains or loses, in such a disadvantaged subgroup, the function he exercised in preliterate society, the fact remains that he continues to be perceived as hero. The reason is probably to be sought in the causes of belief in heroes and heroic ages. C. M. Bowra, in the Earl Grey Memorial Lecture reprinted in *In General and Particular* (London, 1964), pp. 63-84, under the title " The Meaning of a Heroic Age ", lists four of these (pp. 73-80): conquest, exodus, disintegration of an apparently reliable political system, suppression of heroic beliefs by a priestly caste and consequent defiance. The degree to which the last two, and perhaps others as well, were effective in preserving the Nibelungen-material in oral tradition, remains, of course, to be investigated.

and found wanting. The only social stratum, then, which is in a position to perceive verbal irony is the literate stratum, and the only stratum of society which is in a position to regard a " culture hero " as ironic is a stratum for which he is no longer a " culture hero "—i.e. a stratum no longer dependent on the oral epic for the preservation of its cultural identity,—in short, the literate stratum of society. And irony is, of course, a mode not of representation, but of commentary.

Another factor contributes to this change in the perception of an epic entering the realm of literacy. It has been observed that concepts or ideas cannot be expressed as such in oral poetry ; they can only be expressed after transformation into exemplary actions or occurrences in time, and the effectiveness of such expression is directly dependent on certain mnemonic devices which reduce the distance between poet and text, as well as between text and perceiver. These mnemonic devices are not operative in the relationship between written text and reader. The resulting increase in distance between poet, text and perceiver, and the opportunities a stable text offers to the reader to identify or compare non-contiguous segments of narrative with each other, increase the possibilities of perceiving the text as a structure of concepts.

The mere physical situation of reading, or of being read to from a text which is perceived as stable, places the perceiver in a position vis-à-vis the text which is completely different from that of the listener to an oral performance. The social function as well as the mechanics of the oral epic and its recitation require that the perceiver merge with it psychically ; the absence of such merging, i.e. the greater distance between perceiver and stable text conditions a different understanding, an understanding which is also, in part, conditioned by the different function of the text in the different social environment which it enters when it crosses the line into the realm of literacy.[29] In this connection it will be necessary to distinguish between perception and conception: in the former, " the simplest form of perceiving . . . the individual does not clearly distinguish between himself and the external world ", i.e. the stimulus field, in the latter, " the individual observes the external world [i.e. the stimulus field] apart from himself ".[30] Perception and conception, of course, are not pure aspects of cognition, but merely two poles of cognitive continuum. " Somewhere along the continuum ", says Fearing, " symbolic techniques are utilized and I am inclined to think that symbolic techniques and the process of conceptualization must somehow occur coincidentally."[31] With the entry of a narrative into the

[29] Havelock, pp. 197-214, " The Separation of the Knower from the Known ". Cf. also C. M. Bowra's essay, " Some Characteristics of Literary Epic ", in *From Virgil to Milton* (London, 1945), pp. 1-32.

[30] Franklin Fearing in *Language and Culture. Conference on the Interrelations of Language and other Aspects of Culture*, ed. Harry Hoijer (Chicago, 1954), Fourth Session: " The Whorf Hypothesis and Psychological Theory ".

[31] Ibid., pp. 176-177.

area of literacy, the role which symbolism plays in the techniques brought to bear upon it in order to derive meaning from it is sharply increased: it is no longer a matter of the cognition of spoken language—itself, of course, symbolic—but of spoken language rendered in written symbols. The distance between perceiver and text is increased by the addition of another level of symbolism. " In perception the contact is immediate, with a relatively greater opportunity for a feed-back from the stimulus-field ("reality"), which serves as a check on the "accuracy" or appropriateness of the perception. In cognition (or conceptualization) there is a relatively greater opportunity for the operation of interpretive or inferential factors."[32] This additional level of symbolism—writing—brings with it connotations from a realm totally different from that of oral poetry. The "interpretive or inferential factors" operating upon a written text are factors which themselves are not only elicited, but conditioned by literacy, by the cognitive experience with written texts. In the case of medieval literacy, this experience is almost enirely limited to an elucidative rather than a representational system of symbols, and thus augments the distance between text and reader. In short, the oral performance, representative of exemplary deeds, is transformed into a written text, commenting upon a conceptual system. Siegfried arriving at Worms is no longer the hero asserting his might and thereby defining himself as hero, but a political challenge to a political system ; and the quarrel of the queens is no longer an expression of " zweier edelen frouwen nît ", but a confrontation of political order by the capability of an individual to destroy it.

It is only by an application of this and similar historical, sociological, and psycholinguistic data that a text such as that of the *Nibelungenlied* or the *Kudrun* can be analyzed responsibly, i.e. without depriving it of the cultural contexts from which it not only arose but by which it was perceived and given meaning. Since a work of art exists historically only on the basis of its perception, on the basis of the perceived significance arising from the tension between text and " horizons of expectation ", it is essential to establish the factors determining its perception.[33] It is evident that " literacy " and " illiteracy ", written transmission and oral transmission, and their implications as outlined in this paper, are of crucial significance for a determination of the functions of the text, for they not only conditioned the

---

[32] Fearing, " An Examination of the Conceptions of Benjamin Whorf in the Light of Theories of Perception and Cognition ", *Language and Culture*, p. 61. Cf. also pp. 73-78. The connection between literacy and abstraction has long been noted by anthropologists and sociologists, cf. Becker and Barnes, I, 147 ; Havelock, pp. 167, 197, 233. This and the following, of course, give methodological support to such interpretations as those of Siegfried Beyschlag, " Das Motiv der Macht bei Siegfrieds Tod ", *Zur Germanisch-Deutschen Heldensage*, ed. Karl Hauck (Darmstadt, 1961), pp. 195-213, and W. J. Schröder, " Das Nibelungenlied. Versuch einer Deutung ", *BGDSL* (Halle), 76 (1954), 56-143.

[33] Hans Robert Jauss, *Literaturgeschichte als Provokation* (Frankfurt, 1970), pp. 144-207.

immediate perception of the text itself, but also the " horizons of expectation " which determined the understanding of the text.[34]

FRANZ H. BÄUML

*University of California, Los Angeles*

EDDA SPIELMANN

*California State University, Northridge*

[34] Jauss, ibid. One of the more absurd, albeit logical results of attempts to analyze the *Nibelungenlied* without elucidation of the contexts which defined its functions is the necessity of taking refuge in the curious dictum, *ex nihilo*, that the poem was not understood by its public. Cf. D. G. Mowatt and H. Sacker, *The Nibelungenlied: An Interpretative Commentary*, p. 26 ; H. de Boor, *Geschichte der deutschen Literatur* (München, 1964), II, 167 ; Hugo Bekker, *The Nibelungenlied: A Literary Analysis*, p. 4. This is not to say, on the other hand, that we advocate the pursuit of the phantom " understanding of the poem by its contemporary audience " as the ultimate " key " to an " objective meaning " of the poem. Obviously every work of art is perceived and understood differently by different publics at different times. This does not mean that it was *not* understood at any one time. Clearly, responsible criticism must avail itself of all aspects of a poem's function which are reflected in the poem itself and thus can contribute to its elucidation. In the words of Robert M. Adams, ". . . one test of a critical pattern (theory) is its capacity to order in a decisively better way the facts it pretends to control, that is, the text. . . . If the test of the text is not conclusive, we may test in various ways the pattern's relation to the milieu, the tradition, the ambience " (" The Sense of Verification: Pragmatic Commonplaces about Literary Criticism ", *Daedalus*, [Winter 1972], 203-214). And, of course, the " test of the text " can never be conclusive without being perceived in terms emanating from extra-textual realms. If the test of the text of the *Nibelungenlied* were found to be conclusive, there would be no need to deny an understanding of it to any of its audiences—a denial, moreover, which appeals to an environment that the interpreters regard as irrelevant.

# FORMULAIC DICTION IN THE *CANTAR DE MIO CID* AND THE OLD FRENCH EPIC

*In Memoriam*: Karen Zemanek Gilmore

Since Albert B. Lord invoked the metrical irregularity of the *Cantar de mio Cid* as possible evidence that the poem was an orally composed song either " recited for the records " or " taken down by a scribe who does not seek to obtain good rhythmic lines ",[1] several Hispanists have taken up his line of reasoning. L. P. Harvey suggested that the *Cid* may have been performed by a singer who was without his instrument during the recitation whose record we possess in Per Abbat's manuscript.[2] A. D. Deyermond, exploring the implications of such a view, found corroboration for oral composition in the fact that the *Cid* version incorporated into the *Primera Crónica General* accords with Per Abbat's text in the early part of the tale, but deviates progressively as the end approaches, a phenomenon which Lord found in various versions of orally composed Yugoslavian epics and which he explained by observing that the end of a song is sung less frequently than the beginning—and is thus less stable within the tradition—since the singer's performance is often interrupted. Deyermond refused to rule out written composition, however, since, in his view, the characteristics of oral poetry may simply reflect transmission by *juglares* rather than the mode of the poem's creation.[3] Later, analyzing formulas in the *Mocedades de Rodrigo*, Deyermond stressed that both that poem and the *Cid* contain, in addition to the formulas which he considers to be a sign of orality, other elements which he regards as learned.[4] J. M. Aguirre drew a distinction between the *refundición* of a traditional work, essentially a new creation of the type which Parry and Lord found in the Yugoslavian milieu, and the performance of a poem from memory resulting in minor changes such as are found in the Spanish *romance* tradition.[5] A major step toward analysis of the *Cid's* formulas was the publication, in 1968, of Edmund de Chasca's *Registro de*

[1] *The Singer of Tales* (Cambridge: Harvard University Press, 1960), p. 127.

[2] " The Metrical Irregularity of the *Cantar de Mio Cid* ", *Bulletin of Hispanic Studies*, 40 (1963), 137-143.

[3] " The Singer of Tales and Mediaeval Spanish Epic ", *Bulletin of Hispanic Studies*, 42 (1965), 1-8.

[4] *Epic Poetry and the Clergy: Studies on the Mocedades de Rodrigo* (London: Tamesis, 1969), esp. p. 170. In his *A Literary History of Spain: the Middle Ages* (London: Benn, 1971), Deyermond notes, referring to an unpublished study by Margaret Chaplin, that " the use of formulas in the extant Spanish epics is, though too frequent to be the product of mere chance, not frequent enough to indicate oral composition " (p. 40). As will be seen, the research described in the present study leads to another conclusion.

[5] " Epica oral y épica castellana: Tradición creadora y tradición repetitiva ", *Romanische Forschungen*, 80 (1968), 13-43.

*fórmulas verbales en el Cantar de mio Cid*,[6] a listing of expressions occurring three times or more in the poem, constituting 1262 hemistichs, or 17 per cent of the whole. Chasca had assimilated much of the oralists' approach in his *El Arte juglaresco en el Cantar de mio Cid*,[7] the major study of the poem's technique, which includes detailed descriptions of formulaic procedures and characterizes the *Cid* firmly as an example of orally composed literature. He later attempted to adapt Milman Parry's definition of the formula to the peculiar conditions of Old Spanish versification.[8] Stephen Gilman, while appreciating Chasca's essential contributions, noted that the 17 per cent formula density which Chasca found in the *Cid* was not sufficient to place that work in the category of oral poetry according to guidelines adopted by Lord and myself for poems in other national traditions. Although expressing sympathy for the oralists' thesis, Gilman saw that the " attempt to interpret the *Poema* as an oral composition without facing squarely the problems raised by the irregularity of its versification leads to textual doubts so grave as to render meaningless any attempt at critical exegesis ".[9] In the introduction to his important new edition of the *Cid*, Colin Smith devotes considerable attention to the details of oral composition, but ultimately holds that the poem was created " by a thoughtful, cultured individual, in writing ".[10]

Although the theory of oral composition has been accepted by these leading Hispanists—by some as a key to the manner in which the *Cid* was created, by others as a guide to the style characteristics of an orally transmitted text—much of the basic research on formulas in the poem has yet to be published. Some problems have arisen because theoretical conclusions have been drawn before any systematic attempt was made to identify, tabulate, and classify Old Spanish epic formulas. Edmund de Chasca's *Registro* isolates many of the *Cid*'s formulas, but two obstacles prevent total reliance upon it as a research tool. The criteria used in determining just which phrases are formulas are difficult to perceive.[11] In addition, Chasca only includes the phrases which occur three times or more. The distribution of repeated phenomena—be they words or phrases—in a text is such that the largest number are repeated only once, the next largest twice, and so on, with only a few occurring many times. By omitting phrases repeated only once, Chasca eliminated at least one-third of the *Cid*'s formulas from his repertory.

A. D. Deyermond has cautioned that " any observations on formulas in

[6] Iowa City: University of Iowa Press, 1968.

[7] Madrid: Gredos, 1967.

[8] " Toward a Redefinition of the Epic Formula in the Light of the *Cantar de Mio Cid* ", *Hispanic Review*, 38 (1970), 251-263.

[9] " The Poetry of the *Poema* and the Music of the *Cantar* ", *Philological Quarterly*, 51 (1972), 1-11; the quote is from p. 8.

[10] *Poema de mio Cid* (Oxford: Clarendon Press, 1972), p. lvii.

[11] See Gilman, " The Poetry of the *Poema* ", p. 6n.

Spanish epic can only be provisional and tentative until the basic research on the question of oral epic in Spain has been carried out and published ".[12] While progress has been made towards this goal, it will not be reached until all the *Cid*'s formulas have been identified, categorized, and studied.

I have undertaken a full analysis of the *Cid*'s formulaic diction, endeavouring to isolate all hemistichs repeated within the 3761 lines of Colin Smith's edition.[13] Since it is impossible to aspire to a complete list of the *Cid*'s formulas, given the scarcity of *cantares de gesta* which might serve as an adequate basis for comparison, those hemistichs which are repeated within the poem constitute as sure a set of formulas as is feasible under the circumstances. The computer-assisted method which I have employed has been outlined elsewhere,[14] but the irregularity of the *Cid*'s meter compels me to delineate more precisely the parameters of the term " formula " in the context of Old Spanish epic versification before the results of formulaic analysis are set forth.

When Milman Parry articulated his classic definition of the formula, he did so with the Greek dactylic hexameter in mind. Homeric versification is metrically regular, so that when Parry called the formula " a group of words which is regularly employed under the same metrical conditions to express a given essential idea ",[15] the meaning of those " same metrical conditions " was not problematic for him. Nor was it so for researchers in most of the fields in which Parry's ideas were subsequently applied. But for the *Cid*, Menéndez Pidal has found that no one metrical type constituted even as much as one-fifth of the poem's verses.[16] The interpretations of this phenomenon which have been proposed may be reduced to two fundamental options: (1) that the poet composed in a regular versification which was later distorted by transmitters of the text, be they performers or scribes ; or (2) that the poet composed in an irregular meter.[17] Lord's findings in Yugoslavia led L. P. Harvey to propose a further refinement, really a combination of the two options, namely that while the poet may have been accustomed to singing his poem in a regular meter to instrumental accom-

---

[12] *Epic Poetry and the Clergy*, p. 170.

[13] The research was carried out on the basis of Menéndez Pidal's critical text, but the results have been adjusted to conform to the Smith edition, whose readings are less conjectural and less dependent on chronicle versions. To Per Abbat's 3733 lines, Smith adds 29 by restoring the correct division to lines which the copyist erroneously combined ; on the other hand he combines the manuscript's lines 1276 and 1277 into one, for a total of 3761 lines.

[14] *The Song of Roland: Formulaic Style and Poetic Craft* (Berkeley, Los Angeles ; London: University of California Press, 1973), pp. 7-12.

[15] Adam Parry, ed., *The Making of Homeric Verse: the Collected Papers of Milman Parry* (Oxford: Clarendon Press, 1970), p. 272.

[16] *Cantar de mio Cid: texto, gramática y vocabulario* (Madrid: Espasa-Calpe, 1964), I, 99-100. Menéndez Pidal's figures will, of course, have to be revised to take into account the many arbitrary changes which he made in the text, but this fundamental observation will stand.

[17] The latter possibility does not, of course, exclude distortions on the part of the transmitters, leading to further irregularities.

paniment, he did not have his instrument at hand while dictating the version from which Per Abbat's manuscript is descended. According to this hypothesis, only the versification of the written form would have been irregular. Since the *Mocedades de Rodrigo* and the *Roncesvalles* fragment, which with the *Cid* constitute virtually the totality of surviving Old Spanish epic, likewise exhibit extremely irregular versification, one would have to posit in this instance a tradition of dictating without instruments in thirteenth- and fourteenth-century Spain. In any case the irregularity of Old Spanish epic versification is an anomaly within the context of the medieval epic. One naturally expects a sung genre to reflect, in its metrical form, the regularities of song. With this in mind, but without prejudging the still unresolved question of the poem's original metrics, let us examine some potential formula types of the *Cid* whose forms deviate somewhat in their occurrences in the text.

In choosing an expression in which to couch what he has to say, the poet adds or subtracts words which are not essential to the message he wishes to convey. *Amos* in the phrases *saludar nos hemos amos* (2411), *yo e vuestras fijas amas* (1597) and *abiertos amos los braços* (203) is such a superfluous element: cf. *saludar nos hemos* (3030), *yo e vuestras ffijas* (269), and *los braços abiertos* (488). In v. 3030 King Alfonso is speaking to the Cid, so that there are two interlocutors in question just as there are in v. 2411. In vv. 269 and 1597 the *fijas* in question are the Cid's two daughters. Although it is, strictly speaking, redundant for the meaning of these lines, *amos* plays a potentially important role in that it augments the versification by two syllables. The preposition *en* is superfluous in v. 3574, *en essora dixo el rey* (cf. *essora dixo el rey*, 1355, 3416, 3516, 3581, 3668) and in 2380, *en essora dixo mio Cid* (cf. *essora dixo mio Cid*, 3473), as are *yo* in 1696, *entrare yo del otra part* (cf. *entrare del otra part*, 1132) *una* in 3094, *una cofia sobre los pelos* (cf. *cofia sobre los pelos*, 2437), and *todo* in 2684, *que de tod el mundo es señor* (cf. *que del mundo es señor*, 2477, 2493, 2830). *Cras a la mañana* (537, 949) can also be expressed as *cras mañana* (3050), six syllables in the one case, four in the other. The adverbs add little if anything to the sense of 10, *alli pienssan de aguijar* (cf. *e pienssan de aguijar*, 227), 2417, *aqui respuso mio Cid* (cf. *respuso mio Cid*, 2055), 3491, *essora respuso el rey* (cf. *respondio el rey*, 2135, 3042), 2055 ¡*assi lo mande el Criador*! (cf. ¡*el Criador lo mande*! 1404, 1437), 2555, *assi las escarniremos a fijas del Campeador* (cf. *escarniremos las fijas del Campeador*, 2551), or 1142, *e acostar a todas partes los tendales* (cf. *e acostar se los tendales*, 2401). The short form of the hero's name would have sufficed in 819, *dixo Minaya Albar Fañez* (cf. *dixo Minaya*, 1923, 1949), 1297, *oid, Minaya Albar Fañez* (cf. *oid, Minaya*, 810, and *oidme, Minaya*, 1897), and 613, *fablo mio Cid Ruy Diaz* (cf. *fablo mio Cid*, 7, 78, 299, 2036, 2043). An exclamation by the poet is the only difference between the first hemistichs of ¡*Dios, que bien pago a todos sus vassallos*! 806, and ¡*que bien pago a sos vassallos mismos*! 847. A difference in preposition in *enclinaron las caras de suso de los arzones*, 717, adds two syllables to the shorter form *enclinavan las caras sobre los arzones*, 3617. These are only a few examples of gratuitous addition or subtraction of words which fit easily into the context but produce metrical irregularity even within phrases and lines of essentially identical meaning. If the Per Abbat text had been composed in a metrically regular fashion, such sets of lines could easily have been leveled out to a length which would be uniform within each set, and the fact that when there are more than two examples of a given phrase, only one example deviates from the norm, reveals a tendency toward regularity of phrasing. In the *Chanson de Roland* and other Old French texts in which a pentasyllable is required in the first hemistich position and a heptasyllable in the second,[18] similar expansion and contraction of formulas is achieved with identical means, as when *brochent ad ait* (*Roland*, 1184, 1802, 3350, 3541) becomes *brochent amdui a ait* (*Roland*, 1381), or *asez est mielz* (*Roland*, 44, 58, 1518) becomes *si est il asez melz* (*Roland*, 1743). The difference between the two traditions *as we have them in manuscript* is that this metrical flexibility allows the *Roland* poet to adapt his formulas to the anisosyllabic hemistich positions, whereas in the *Cid* it produces metrical irregularity in phrases which would otherwise correspond to Parry's " group of words which is regularly employed under the same metrical conditions. . . ."

A complementary phenomenon is apparent in certain phrases which vary metrically with a change in tense. *Assi lo fazen todos* (2488) is heptasyllabic, *assi lo an todos ha far* (322) enneasyllabic *agudo*, and *assi ffagamos nos todos* (3728) enneasyllabic *llano*. Similarly *por que las han dexadas* (3278) is heptasyllabic, but *por que las dexamos* (3299) has one syllable less. In the French tradition, poets have ways of compensating for tense changes. Thus *les enchalcerent Franc* (*Roland*, 1660), a formula in the *passé simple*, becomes *ben les enchalcent Franc* (*Roland*, 2460) in the present tense. This process of metrical compensation is susceptible of two interpretations: either the French poet wished to emphasize, through addition of the adverb *ben*, the zeal with which the knights in question engaged in their pursuit of the enemy forces, or he wanted to employ the present tense and added the adverb because of metrical considerations. A conjunction of the two reasons is not to be ruled out. But while the purpose is obscure, the phenomenon of flexibility is clear. Once again one can perceive the utility of the process in the French tradition, where it is subordinated to the needs of rhythm, but in the Spanish it has contributed to a lack of the metrical uniformity one normally expects of sung poetry.

Are the variations within the sets of phrases discussed thus far sufficiently great that the anomalous hemistichs should be denied the qualification " formula " ? I can see two answers to this question, both of which are

[18] I use here the Spanish conventions for describing versification, a pentasyllable designating a four-syllable hemistich with optional post-tonic fifth syllable, and a heptasyllable a six-syllable hemistich with optional post-tonic seventh syllable.

valid within a certain context. In a sense the phrases are all formulas, because even when the poet or scribe who is responsible for their present form added or subtracted words, the essential pattern is still visible to the modern critic, and presumably was perceived by their author. On the other hand, there is a degree of variation beyond which reasonable minds will not admit the similarity of varying phrases, and the hemistichs which approach that limit weaken the evidence for formulaic composition. A practical consideration—namely the availability of data for formula densities in the Old French epic, compiled under clearly defined criteria—leads me to adopt, for the purposes of this study, a set of rather narrow parameters for the formula. All hemistichs included within the set limits will indeed be formulas, although some other phrases not included within them are counted by other critics as formulas for intuitive reasons, and sometimes rightly so.[19] The resulting data will be comparable with the figures for formula density in the eleventh, twelfth, and thirteenth-century French epics which have been studied elsewhere, because both analyses will be based upon the same criteria as nearly as that is possible given the difference in metrics between the cognate bodies of epic.

Only hemistichs which recur within the *Cid* will be counted as formulas, and by recurring hemistichs I mean those whose principal words are identical (nouns, attributive adjectives, verbs), even when those words do not occur in the same order (as, for example, *plega al Criador*, 2149, 2892, and *al Criador plega*, 2100) or when the hemistichs represent different metrical values. For example, to use some phrases already discussed, *cras mañana* and *cras a la mañana* will be counted as two instances of the same formula,

[19] Thus in a chapter entitled " Procedimientos formularios de la narración ", Edmund de Chasca includes *pareçen los alvores* as an instance of the formula *e quieren crebar albores* and calls *el día es salido, e la noch es entrada* a variant of *el día es exido, la noch querié entrar*. See his *El Arte juglaresco*, pp. 211-212. Chasca's definition of the formula, elaborated in his book and in " Toward a Redefinition of the Epic Formula in the Light of the *Cantar de Mio Cid* ", *Hispanic Review*, 38 (1970), 251-263, calls for comment. He proposes: " A formula is a habitual device of style or of narrative mode: as verbal expression it is a group of words forming an identical or variable pattern which is used in the same, or similar, or dissimilar metrical conditions to express a given essential idea whose connotative meaning is frequently determined by the extent to which it is modified by poetic context ; as narrative mode, it refers to the customary but variable manner in which the verbal matter is arranged to tell a story ". (" Toward a Redefinition ", pp. 257-258.) This definition rests upon the assumption that what we have in the Per Abbat manuscript is not the scribal deformation of metrically regular formulas, but rather the formulas themselves, a question which I would rather leave open for the present. There is little if anything in any epic, written or oral, which would not qualify as a " habitual device of style or of narrative mode ". Furthermore, that the formula's meaning is in some way modified by the poetic context was not denied by Parry. Connotation is, however, a matter of function and semantic nuance rather than of definition. The " customary but variable manner in which the verbal matter is arranged to tell a story " is an important aspect of the oral poet's technique, but to employ the term " formula " to characterize it is to dilute the word's meaning and cloud its uses at a time when one should be trying to render it more precise. Chasca leans toward the terminological usage of C. M. Bowra, whom I find to be the least rigorous of the oral theorists. Certainly Bowra's statement that formulas are most frequent when the poet lacks talent or when he has to sing without sufficient time to prepare his performance (see *El Arte juglaresco*, p. 168) is highly questionable.

as will be *por que las dexamos* and *por que las han dexadas, entrare del otra part* and *entrare yo del otra part.* *Dixo Minaya Albar Fañez*, on the other hand, will not be included as a variation of *dixo Minaya* (which itself does qualify since it occurs twice in that form). ¡*Que bien pago!* will not be counted with ¡*Dios, que bien pago!* nor will *essora respuso el rey* with *respondio el rey.* This distinction may seem arbitrary to some, and to a certain degree it is, but no more so than any distinction one might choose. It has a definite merit: the syntactic flexibility of the formula resides largely in its function words (conjunctions, prepositions, interjections, definite and indefinite articles, possessive or demonstrative adjectives), while its utility as an element which conveys a message is in the words which carry the meaning of Parry's " given essential idea ". Thus an insistence on identity of those words which carry the semantic weight of the formula, coupled with a tolerance for variation in the function words, retains the essence of Parry's definition. An exception to this rule has been allowed, namely phrases occurring in the second hemistich position which would be identical within the guidelines adopted except for the words occurring at the assonance, in cases where those words are semantically equivalent: for example *el burgales complido* (65), *un burgales contado* (193), *un burgales leal* (1459), phrases which differ from *el burgales de pro* (736, 2837, 3066, 3191) only because of the needs of assonance. In this instance it is noteworthy that the same variations occur in another set of formulas: *el Campeador [conplido]* (69), *el Campeador contado* (142 [*al*], 152 [*del*], 493 [*Campeador contado*], 1780, 2433), *el Campeador leal* (396, 2361b [*Canpeador leal*], 2679 [*al*], 3317 [*al*]).[20] The exception made in counting such hemistichs as formulas has affected the final figures very little.[21]

Finally, let me anticipate the possible objection that Spanish formulas of varying metrical values are not comparable with the metrically regular Old French formulas by pointing out that formulas of differing lengths do occur in the decasyllable *chanson de geste*, where first hemistich formulas are tetrasyllabic while those found in the second hemistich are hexasyllabic.[22]

For the present I prefer to leave aside the question of syntactic formulas and formula systems, although there can be no doubt that they are of capital importance in the performance of any oral poem. Syntactic formula systems are more likely to be obscured by the processes which make for metrical irregularity in the *Cid* than are semantic formulas, and thus are less useful as a test for formulaic composition. I will confine myself here to the semantic

[20] Such variation is occasionally achieved through transposition, as well as by tense change: *e los buenos que i ha* (3058), *de los buenos que i son* (3072) ; *mio natural señor* (2031), *mio señor natural* (1272). Both of these types would have been counted as formulas in any case.

[21] Only thirteen phrases have been considered to be formulas which otherwise would not have qualified. I have only counted them in order to insure comparability with the figures for French formulas. where such assonantal variations play a greater role.

[22] French terminology.

formula, as I did in the study of the *Chanson de Roland* considered within the context of Old French epic and romance.

My research shows the presence of 2385 semantic formulas in the Per Abbat text, constituting 31.7 per cent of its 7522 hemistichs. In the following table, this figure is compared to the hemistichs repeated within each of thirteen Old French epics and romances which were analyzed according to the same criteria. The French epic line is divided into two hemistichs, of equal length in the case of works written in alexandrines, of unequal length if they are composed in decasyllabic verse.[23] The percentage figures are rounded to the nearest unit.

| Poem | Percentage of repeated hemistichs | Approximate date | Versification |
|---|---|---|---|
| *Buevon de Conmarchis* | 15 | 1269-1285 | dodecasyllabic |
| *Roman d'Enéas* | 16 | 1150-1160 | octosyllabic |
| *Roman d'Alexandre* | 17 | 1150 | decasyllabic |
| *Pèlerinage de Charlemagne* | 23 | 1100 | dodecasyllabic |
| *Siège de Barbastre* | 23 | 1180 | decasyllabic |
| *Moniage Guillaume* | 24 | 1180 | decasyllabic |
| *Gormont et Isembart* | 29 | 1068-1104 | octosyllabic |
| *Charroi de Nîmes* | 29 | 1135-1165 | decasyllabic |
| *Chanson de Guillaume* | 31 | 1075-1125 | decasyllabic |
| *Cantar de mio Cid* | 32 | 1207 | ? |
| *Raoul de Cambrai* | 33 | 1190 | decasyllabic |
| *Chanson de Roland* | 35 | 1095-1100 | decasyllabic |
| *Couronnement de Louis* | 37 | 1131-1150 | decasyllabic |
| *Prise d'Orange* | 39 | 1150-1165 | decasyllabic |

In relation to the ten *chansons de geste*, the *Cid* is situated slightly above the median: it is more formulaic than six of the French epics, less formulaic than four.

No correlation was found between formulaic density and either date of composition or type of versification in the French material. There is, however, a marked distinction between the *chansons de geste* and the courtly romances *Enéas* and *Alexandre*, works whose written nature no one disputes and which were used as controls. The author of the derivative *Buevon de Conmarchis*,[24] Adenet le Roi, also wrote *Cléomades*, a romance, as well as two other imitations of *chansons de geste*: *Berte aus grans piés* and *Les Enfances Ogier*. He was a learned author, and the position of *Buevon de Conmarchis*

[23] French terminology. In the octosyllabic epic *Gormont et Isembart*, the hemistichs are sometimes isosyllabic, sometimes anisosyllabic.

[24] *Buevon de Conmarchis* is based on a lost manuscript of *Le Siège de Barbastre* which Adenet claims to have obtained at the Abbey of Saint Denis. *Buevon's* plot corresponds to the first 2700 lines of J.-L. Perrier's edition of *Le Siège de Barbastre* (Paris: Champion, 1926).

at the low end of the table confirms the stylistic distinction between works known to have been composed in writing on the one hand, and the *chanson de geste* on the other, a distinction which the *Cid*'s placement on the table does nothing to dispel. The romances average 16 per cent in repeated hemistichs, while the *chansons de geste* taken as a whole are 30.3 per cent formulaic.[25] The *Cid* is, then, slightly more formulaic than the average of ten eleventh and twelfth-century French epics.

Formulaic analysis is a matter of comparative proportions. The simple presence of repeated hemistichs reveals nothing about the manner in which a work was composed or transmitted, since any writer is capable of repeating himself and since indeed repetition is difficult and perhaps even impossible to avoid in long poetic works. Even a high proportion of formulas would not indicate oral composition or transmission, were there no evidence for significantly lower levels of repetition in a narrative genre whose works are known to have been created in writing. But a consistent difference in repetition between two genres is another question, especially when some scholars have been proposing that long narrative poems can be composed without the aid of writing implements by means of a stylized system of repetitions, and that systematic repetition is conversely a sign of orality. I have conjectured that the threshold of semantic formula density below which one should conclude that a work was composed in writing is 20 per cent.[26] As the figure rises above that level, the probability of orality increases. The *Cid*, with 31.7 per cent formulas, is solidly within the range of oral poetry.

How is this figure to be reconciled with Chasca's result of 17 per cent formula density in the *Cid*? Chasca did not count all the formulas, but only those occurring three times or more. Since my research shows that 417 formula types occur only twice each, for a total of 834 occurrences, this difference in scope would account for most of the variance between the two percentages. The rest would represent a difference in criteria. Unfortunately Chasca's criteria are nowhere delineated, so that I cannot compare them with mine. I am, however, prepared to defend the ones I have adopted as valid for quantitative studies. They are the result of long deliberation. In any case, the comparison of the *Cid* with the *chansons de geste* would be little affected by any difference between Chasca's criteria and my own, since mine were applied without deviation to both Spanish and French texts.

The significance of the *Cid*'s formula density cannot be adequately assessed unless one relates it to the results of other literary and historical research, a project which is beyond the scope of the present study. Furthermore, formula density is but one aspect—although perhaps the most important—of the poem's stylistic profile. Topics such as the distribution of

[25] For a more detailed discussion, see *The Song of Roland: Formulaic Style and Poetic Craft*, pp. 21-30.

[26] *The Song of Roland: Formulaic Style and Poetic Craft*, pp. 29-30.

formulas within the *Cid*, the use of those formulas for thematic purposes,[27] the relationship between formulas and metrical irregularity, remain to be elucidated more fully. But even before these questions are treated, a tentative conclusion might be drawn. Lord found an inverse correlation between literacy and oral composition in twentieth-century Yugoslavia, and if, in the absence of sociological data concerning medieval *juglares*, we are to accept his research as indicative of a universal disjunction between singers of tales and literate culture, then the *Cid*'s formula density would seem to corroborate Menéndez Pidal's contention, recently subjected to reconsideration,[28] that the *Cid* was the creation of a functionally unlettered poet. Evidence for the poet's acquaintance with chronicles, law, documents, and chancery practice is insufficient to mark him as learned insofar as the creation of his poem is concerned. Whole societies, such as Iceland in the early middle ages, are known to have functioned under a system of orally transmitted law. Even if the poet shows a knowledge of chronicles, documents, and diplomatics, even if he was literate to the extent of employing reading and writing for official purposes—which is by no means certain—, the relatively high formula density of the *Cid* certainly indicates that he did not compose his poem in a way typical of the creative habits of literate poets.

JOSEPH J. DUGGAN

*University of California, Berkeley*

---

[27] See Chasca, *El Arte juglaresco*, pp. 165-216.

[28] See Deyermond, *History*, pp. 44-45, and C. C. Smith, " Latin Histories and Vernacular Epic in Twelfth-Century Spain: Similarities of Spirit and Style ", *Bulletin of Hispanic Studies*, 48 (1971), 1-19. A treatment of references to documents is found in P. E. Russell, " Some Problems of Diplomatic in the *Cantar de mio Cid* and their Implications ", *Modern Language Review*, 47 (1952), 340-349.

# ORAL COMPOSITION AND THE PERFORMANCE OF NOVELS OF CHIVALRY IN SPAIN

From the ways in which contemporaries spoke of the prose narrator I am going to describe, it is clear that he was in his day regarded as an exceptional individual. He was a member of a culturally backward-looking community, the Moriscos,[1] and so he may well represent the continuation into the later sixteenth century of cultural features of great antiquity. On the other hand it could well be that the Morisco family to which he belonged constituted, as it were, a fresh (and irrelevant) cultural mutation rather than a throwback to an earlier state. On these matters we can only speculate, but the implications of this particular case are so far-reaching that any student of the relations between oral and popular literature cannot fail to bear it in mind.

Students of Cervantes, in particular, will certainly look at *Don Quijote*[2] in a new perspective in the light of the extraordinary similarities (which Julio Caro Baroja[3] has already pointed out) between the case of this Morisco, author of novels of chivalry, protegé of a duke, alleged rider on a magic flying horse, and Cervantes' masterpiece, published only five years after the Inquisition trial which is our only source of information about the Morisco " author ".

*The dossier on a sixteenth-century oral entertainer:*
*the extraordinary case of Román Ramírez*

The Morisco quack doctor, herbalist and public story-teller Román Ramírez was arrested near Soria by order of the Inquisition on October 27, 1595. He died in custody on December 8, 1599, and some ten weeks after his death, was found guilty by the Inquisition of a number of offences ranging from witchcraft to apostasy. He was posthumously included in an *auto de fe* which took place in Toledo in the Zocodover before Philip III on March 5, 1600. His story is not unknown to some specialist students of Spanish

---

[1] There has been considerable activity in the field of research into Morisco life and culture in recent years, but H. C. Lea, *The Moriscos of Spain, their conversion and expulsion*, London 1901, reprint 1968, remains a fundamental work. For cultural history, see my unpublished Oxford thesis, *The Literary Culture of the Moriscos, 1492-1609*, 2 vols., presented at Oxford, 1958. Amongst the most recent works see Louis Cardaillac, *La polémique antichrétienne des morisques ou l'opposition de deux communautés*, 3 vols., Montpellier, Université Paul Valéry, 1973 and Denise Cardaillac, *La polémique anti-chrétienne du manuscrit aljamiado no. 4944 de la bibliothèque national de Madrid*, 2 vols., Montpellier, 1972.

[2] In the introduction to his edition of *Don Quijote* published by Editorial Magisterio Español, Madrid, 1971, Américo Castro (vol. 1, pp. 28-29) summarizes his arguments for supposing that the novel reflects the forgery by the Moriscos of the apocryphal scriptures usually known as the Sacromonte lead tablets (*libros plúmbeos*). I do not consider this hypothesis to be in conflict with the hypothesis advanced by Caro Baroja (see n. 3), rather I see the two approaches as being complementary.

[3] J. Caro Baroja, *Vidas mágicas e inquisición*, 2 vols., Madrid, 1967, especially vol. 1, pp. 309-328.

culture, to students of the drama in particular, but I am not aware that his fascinating biography has hitherto been analysed for the unexpected light which it throws on the obscure period of transition between oral entertainments, the oral art of the medieval *joculatores* and storytellers on one hand, and, on the other, that of the authors of such written prose entertainments as the novels of chivalry.

Our only reliable source of information about this Morisco is the thick dossier (*legajo*) assembled by the Inquisition for the trial in Cuenca and still preserved quite intact and in excellent condition in the diocesan archive in the Bishop's Palace there.[4] It is true that in the early seventeenth century a Jesuit, Martín del Río,[5] writing on the subject of magic refers to some aspects of the affair in not inconsiderable detail. Unless del Río had access to the Inquisition documentation, he must have picked up the tales which would have circulated in Toledo, and indeed in the court, as a result of the *auto de fe*.

Basing himself on some contemporary sources too, but drawing in large measure on his imagination and on his knowledge of the sort of themes which appealed to playgoers of the period, Juan Ruiz de Alarcón wrote a *comedia, Quien mal anda en mal acaba*, of which the villain is a wicked Morisco called Román Ramírez. The action takes place in Deza, where the real-life Morisco of this name had his permanent residence. The play was certainly not written very long after the death of Román Ramírez, although Alarcón scholars[6] disagree as to the exact date of composition. Fernández-Guerra, followed by Millares Carlo, thinks that it was written in 1617, whereas Castro Leal thinks it earlier: from between 1601 and 1603. The earlier date would seem likely if the play were written under the impulse of the *auto de fe* itself, the later one if, as is more likely, the inspiration were Martín del Río's book. In any case this play is in no way a reliable source of information, although it does contain vestigial traces of the facts which will interest us below.

M. Menéndez y Pelayo included a brief one-paragraph reference to Román Ramírez in his *Historia de los heterodoxos españoles*[7] on the basis of what is

---

[4] I would like to express my gratitude to the bishop and chapter of Cuenca who kindly permitted me to consult these papers in 1971 at a time clearly most inconvenient to themselves.

[5] Martín del Río, *Disquisitionum magicarum*, libri sex, Venice, 1616, pp. 198-210, quoted by Caro Baroja, see n. 3 above. On Martín del Río see also J. Caro Baroja, *El señor inquisidor y otras vidas por oficio*, Madrid, 1968, chapter 6, pp. 171-245.

[6] On Juan Ruiz de Alarcón see Walter Poesse, *Ensayo de una bibliografía de J. Ruiz de Alarcón y Mendoza*, Valencia, 1964. No. 298 lists only one seventeenth-century edition of the play *Quien mal anda en mal acaba*: the undated one produced by Francisco de Leefdael in Seville. Millares Carlo discusses the dating of the play in his edition of Juan Ruiz de Alarcón, *Obras completas*, III, Mexico, 1968, see especially p. 169. A. E. Foley naturally treats *Quien mal anda . . .* in *Occult arts and doctrine in the theater of Juan Ruiz de Alarcón*, Geneva, 1972, but is concerned with general ideas rather than with the specific details of the Inquisition trial.

[7] Marcelino Menéndez Pelayo, *Historia de los heterodoxos españoles*, I refer to the edition in Biblioteca de autores cristianos, Madrid, 1956, vol. II, pp. 310-11.

to be found in Alarcón and Martín del Río. The deadpan and noncommittal manner of Menéndez y Pelayo's delivery makes it difficult to determine whether irony was intended or not, but I cannot find any in the final sentence reporting complacently that " Ejercitaba indistintamente su ciencia en maleficiar y en curar maleficios, hasta que por sus jactancias imprudentes descubrieron el juego y la Inquisición de Toledo le prendió y castigó en 1600 ". As later will be seen, this is in no way accurate, and we may safely ignore Menéndez y Pelayo's tendentious contribution.

The fundamental study on the subject of this Morisco is due to A. González Palencia who in 1929-1930 published in the *Boletín de la Real Academia Española* an article reprinted in his volume *Historias y Leyendas, estudios literarios*[8] under the title of "El curandero morisco del siglo XVI, Román Ramírez ". This is based on the discovery which González Palencia had made in the archives at Cuenca of the Inquisition dossier mentioned above. González Palencia is thus able for the first time to set out what part of Alarcón's *comedia* is drawn from events which occurred, or are alleged to have occurred, in the late sixteenth century, and to what extent his Román Ramírez is a creation of fiction. But far more important even than this, we are given copious summaries of the dossier, and quotations permitting us to form some ideas of the psychological complexities of this extraordinary individual.

The chapter entitled ' Magia y estilazación literaria. Un hechizero morisco Román Ramírez. (Realidad y ficción en su derredor) ' in Julio Caro Baroja's study *Vidas Mágicas e Inquisición* (see n. 3 above) is without doubt the most penetrating analysis of the psychology of the historical personage Román Ramírez and also of the accretions of myth and fiction which grew up round him. Textually it is based on González Palencia and Martín del Río. Caro Baroja has, of course, all the range of modern conceptual tools of the anthropologist at his disposal.

For the present study I went back to the Inquisition papers themselves in Cuenca. I did not do this because of any mistrust on my part of González Palencia's readings. (In fact I found him a reliable guide through the crabbed impenetrabilities of sixteenth-century legal hands.) González Palencia had been interested in Román Ramírez primarily as a man, as a *curandero*, as a source of Alarcón's play. He devotes only six pages to Román as a *story-teller* accused of truck with the Devil because he was able to perform extraordinary feats of memory. It is on the contrary this side of Román Ramírez which concerns me most. We know almost nothing of the inner life and the creative process of the oral performer. In studies of oral epic and oral narrative the man who recites or sings or narrates recedes into anonymity. He is seen as a type, not as an individual. In the eyes of some he becomes merely a mouthpiece through which the voice of some mysterious abstraction such as the People speaks. Our ignorance of the story-teller is largely due to the fact that his contemporaries were less interested in him that in his wares.

[8] A. González Palencia, *Historias y leyendas*, Madrid, 1942, pp. 215-284.

Turoldus (if the *geste* was indeed his creation) little realised how much ink would eventually be spilt over his name! And our ignorance of personal characteristics is paralleled by ignorance with regard to the techniques of composition as seen from the point of view of the composer or performer. These Inquisition papers do something to lift one corner of that veil. They do so because the Morisco, under the terrible stress of the inquisitorial procedure, found it expedient to blurt out his trade secrets, to show how the apparently miraculous technical effects of story-telling which he was able to achieve were all subject to a perfectly human, and not to a supernatural, explanation.

## The Dossier

The documents which González Palencia tracked down in the 1920's in the diocesan archive at Cuenca bore in his day the identification *Procesos del Siglo XVI No. 86*, but since then the inquisitional papers have been resorted (presumably by Cirac[9]), and the item bears the classification leg.(ajo) 343 No. 4876. A number of documents in distinct hands on different types and sizes of paper have been bound up to form a volume, the leaves of which were not originally numbered, but which has in recent years received a pencil foliation, so that we now have a title page followed by a single blank sheet followed by 262 folios of various sizes. Some of the documents are very clearly written in Renascence hands, others in difficult legal hands, and some are of ill-prepared paper which has absorbed over the years a great deal of ink.

The title page reads:

Proceso contra Roman Ramirez morisco vezino y natural de la villa de Deça, obispado de Siguenza, 1595 (Letrado, el licenciado Collado).

A further note on the title page reads:

Murio en 8 de diziembre de 1599 año como consta por una carta del licenciado Sanchez y esta al fin del legajo.

Relaxado en estatua y exhumado sus huesos y llevado a Toledo donde se executo su sentencia por comision del Sr. Cardenal Guevara, Inquisidor General, como consta por la pronunciacion de su sentencia.

There is on the title page a summary table of contents, but it does not refer to the folio numbers (which are, as has been explained, modern) and simply gives the general order in which documents appear:

Acusación ; Prueba ; murió en este estado ; curandería ; publicación ; concluso por diffa[mación]. Of more use as guides through the various documents are the not infrequent marginal notes which, in the manner of the period, call attention to salient points of interest.

From the documents it is possible to piece together the story of the accused man's life. González Palencia and Caro Baroja have already done this, but it will be helpful to rehearse the facts here, filling in some details

---

[9] S. Cirac Estopiñán, *Registros de los documentos del Santo Oficio de Cuenca y Sigüenza*, tomo 1, Registro General de los procesos de delitos y de los expedientes de limpieza, Cuenca-Barcelona, 1965, p. 291, nᵒ 4876.

from the additional material, There subsist minor uncertainties with regard to some dates in Román's life, and this is indeed not surprising since these were days when in many families men were content to know merely their approximate age, and the exact date of birth was of interest, if at all, for astrological rather than for administrative reasons. What is more, Román Ramírez was a Morisco, a member of a group which hovered confusedly between the incompatible Muslim and Christian calendars. I have had occasion in my researches into other papers written by Moriscos themselves to check the equivalences between Christian and *ḥijrī* datings which are sometimes provided by Morisco scribes: they are often erroneous. We must not therefore expect strict chronological accuracy in the evidence we are examining. In addition we must remember that the evidence was produced to Inquisition tribunals in which the strict rules of procedure, by removing familiar frames of reference, were only too likely to disorientate and confuse the witnesses.

Nevertheless, a chronology can be established with a probability of error which one may guess as being no greater than $\pm$ 5 years at any point, and there are fixed points such as the date of arrest (1595), death, of course, (1599) and also an earlier set of inquisitional proceedings in 1571 when the Morisco was given benefit of an edict of grace after confessing that he had lapsed back into Islamic ways.

### The Life of Román Ramírez

Román was described as being about thirty when the Inquisition first interested themselves in him in 1571, and as about sixty during his trial 1595-1599. One may therefore suppose him to have been born in 1535-1540. One must bear in mind that at this time the Morisco community had only just come into being, throughout the Middle Ages there had been native *Muslim* communities in all parts of Spain except the extreme north and north-west, and what modern historians call the Moriscos (and what contemporaries more usually termed *nuevos convertidos de moros*) came into being when these native Muslims were by edict forced to adopt Christianity. This is not the place to go into the problem of knowing when this step took place, and indeed much research has still to be done to determine when exactly the conversion was actually imposed in particular areas. In general terms the lands subject to the crown of Castile were converted in the aftermath of the first rebellion in Granada 1500-1501, whereas the dependencies of the crown of Aragón did not experience conversion until the upheavals accompanying and following on the *germania* movement in Valencia: i.e. the mid-1520's. Deza stands on the frontier between Castile and Aragón, belonging administratively and ecclesiastically on the Castilian side of the border, so that we may assume that in theory at least the conversion was applied there at the beginning of the sixteenth century. He is described by one witness (Licenciado Bonifaz) as " a Morisco of those of Castile ", i.e.

not a recent Granadan immigrant, but Román Ramírez was related to Moriscos from the Aragonese side of the border, his mother, María de Luna, herself " well versed in medical matters " being the daughter of an Aragonese Morisco well-known in the region for his medical skills: Juan de Luna. We must therefore think of Román Ramírez growing up in a community which had just undergone the shock of forced conversion. It is known that in many cases " conversion " was a purely outward show, and indeed Moriscos were advised by their religious leaders that under duress they could quite properly " bow down to idols " and transgress Muslim teachings (including that against drinking wine and eating pork). There came into being a special crypto-Muslim mentality, a pattern of deeply contradictory behaviour. The contradictions of the life of Román Ramírez are not surprising, springing as they do from such a background. Román Ramírez's life spanned the period which stretched from the early years of the forced conversions to the end of the century, when the Christians had become exasperated to realise that the insincere conversion which they had forced on these Muslims was doomed for ever to remain insincere. Less than ten years after Román Ramírez died the edict of expulsion was decreed. It is profoundly sad to trace in his life the way in which beliefs and behaviour which would have passed as quite unremarkable only a century earlier brought in Counter-Reformation Spain persecution, imprisonment and death.

Román Ramírez's father bore exactly the same name as he did. He is described as a cultivator (*labrador*). The boy appears to have been brought up in the house of his maternal grandfather where he began to acquire an education. Whether the story that the grandfather had administered camphor to him in order to " dry out his brain " so as to give him a good memory, is true, it was there as a boy that he heard books read and presumably began to exercise the memory which was later to win him such a reputation. One may presume that it was in the bosom of his family that he was initiated into Muslim rites and beliefs. The story which Román tells the Inquisitors was that he was thirteen or fourteen when a servant in the house of his father, one Jerónimo de Villaverde from Terrer (already in the *Poema de Mio Cid*[10] a village of Moors) instructed him when to fast Ramadán. This was no doubt a story to try to ward off the attentions of the Inquisition from the family as such. He confessed that for the next four or five years he kept the fast.

In about 1558 he went to live in Teruel with Angela de Miranda, his first wife, by whom he had three children. It may have been about this time that he learned to read. Evidence on his literacy is somewhat contradictory, since he states he could not write, and yet claims to have been paid 300

---

[10] Mentions of Terrer as being inhabited by Moors come in the Alcocer episode (lines 557 ss) ; the place Alcocer has never been identified, nor have Fáriz and Galve, the Moorish leaders in the final battle (656 ss.). This incident is probably a piece of juglaresque invention, but there is no reason to doubt the reality of Ateca, Terrer and Calatayud (lines 625-6) as Muslim centres of resistance to the Cid's movements in this area.

reales for " writing " a book of chivalry. He states (f. 202) that he could read but little and did not know how to write, only to sign his name. He claimed that he taught himself to read thirty years before his second trial (i.e. about 1558) after being taught the letters by a child from an alphabet book. On the other hand, both his grandfather and his father could read well, and he speaks of hearing them read, so it is difficult to see why reading came to him so late and in such a fashion. Certainly when the Inquisitors tested his reading in 1598 they found it clumsy and slow.

It must have been about 1558 that he acquired a copy of Dioscorides,[11] which he confessed to buying in Madrid. Perhaps the practical advantages of being able to make out this text for his medical work spurred him on. He was at this period inheriting the reputation as a healer which his grandfather had won, and, for example, in 1563 was called to Calatayud to treat one Carlos López. In his religious life he was not keeping up the fast of Ramadán, because of his ignorance of the correct dates (and not, presumably, out of any preference for Christianity).

A brawl in Deza, during which he became involved in a knife-fight with one Licenciado Páez, led him to flee from the region, and he went as an agricultural labourer across the provincial border to reap at the house of Juan de Fuentes, and there he once again began to fast, but he swung back to Christianity again in 1570-1571, when he confessed and was included in the " general pardon " accorded to the Moriscos of Deza as part of the evangelistic effort being made at that time (as a consequence of the second Granadan War).

At the time of his inclusion in the " general pardon " his first wife was still alive. His second wife, Ana de Ucedo, bore him two children and she was still alive during the Inquisition proceedings which led to his death. Román claims that he continued as a good Christian for about twenty years until a Turkish slave called Muçali came to Deza and tempted him back to Muslim practices in about 1588.

Quite apart from his religious vacillations, his public status was contradictory. At the time of his arrest he was clearly an influential man within his own community, for he was " alcalde de ordinario " of the Moriscos of Deza: we may presume that the Christian authorities found it expedient to appoint a Morisco official to ensure the co-operation of the Morisco inhabitants. On the other hand, in about 1590 he had been in prison in Medinaceli. He was a man with powerful friends and powerful enemies. The Christian inhabitants of Deza had a grudge against him because he was a member of the Duke of Medinaceli's party. Licentiate Bonifaz disliked him because of an affray he had with Pedro de Barrionuevo. And no doubt as a result of

[11] This would have been Laguna's translation: Pedacio Dioscorides Anazarbeo, *Acerca de la materia medicinal y de los veneos mortiferos, traduzido . . . & illustrado con claras y substantiales Annotationes y con las figuras de innumeras plantas exquisitas y raras,* por el Doctor Andrés de Laguna. The British Museum possesses an Antwerp edition of 1555 and Salamanca editions of 1566 and 1570.

one of these feuds Román's son was killed not long before the trial: the old man found his son's body in the fields outside the town.

Román's ill-fated visit to Soria to recite novels of chivalry to entertain Pedro Ramírez and his guest Gil Ramírez de Arellano, *oidor* (judge) of Valladolid, took place in 1595. Pedro Ramírez, having summoned Román from a great distance to entertain his influential guests, naturally was not inclined to yield precedence when the corregidor of Soria, Iñigo de Orozco, insisted that *he* wanted to have Román recite in his house that same night. When it appeared to Orozco that he was not going to get his way, and thus risked losing face, he spitefully deprived the Ramírezs of their entertainment by giving to the Inquisition information concerning an alleged offence of witchcraft committed by Román in Tagajuerce. The " offence " appears at this distance in time to have been in the nature of an amateur faith-healing cure of a bad case of psychological maladjustment in marriage. The details are interesting enough in themselves, and one would note that psychiatrists would find a rich mine of information on abnormal behaviour of all kinds in the Inquisition papers, but this does not concern us for our present purposes, and it suffices that Orozco had sufficient pretext to have Román arrested. Once he was in the hands of the Inquisition, of course, the rules of procedure placed no end term to the probing, and all the multifarious facts and fantasies of the old man's life were raked over and assembled into the dossier which survives today.

Román tried to flee, but was captured. He was sent to the Inquisition's prison at Cuenca, presumably because his permanent residence at Deza fell within the diocese of Sigüenza, and Sigüenza depended for purposes of the Inquisition on Cuenca. In Cuenca Román was far from home and friends. It was not possible for him to receive gifts of food, as could have been arranged if he had been closer to his family, and he suffered greatly. He was no doubt worn out already by a hard life, and four years of the dreadful suspense of the procedure of the tribunal of the Holy Office was enough to reduce him to such a state that even his hard jailers had him transferred to hospital. There they tried to extract information by having one of the nurses ingratiate herself. They were not at this stage seeking further facts with regard to his heresy—they presumably had more than enough to burn him. They were convinced that the old man had a hidden treasure, and they were on the alert to discover where he had buried it. (Readers of *Don Quixote* will call to mind the Moor Ricote who came back to Spain disguised as a German in order to dig up the treasure he had buried [Part II ch. LIV]: Spaniards at this time were obsessed with the idea the Moriscos had hidden resources.) Of all the sad story of the treatment of Román Ramírez, there is no part which is more disgraceful than this sordid last phase in the Hospital de Santiago in Cuenca. Román died on December 8th, 1599.

Death did not, of course, close the dossier, and the tribunal proceeded, with perhaps some haste, to try the case in the following month: the vote condemning him was taken on February 13th. The reason for this haste, when the whole affair had been allowed to drag on for more than four years, was that once the man was dead there was no hope of extracting information from him ; there was advantage in getting the case completed tidily so that Román could be included in an *auto de fe* being prepared in Toledo for March 5th. It was a spectacular affair presided over by that Inquisitor General Cardinal Niño de Guevara, of whom such a striking portrait by El Greco exists in the Metropolitan Museum, New York. The King, Philip III, was present. Román, who claimed to have entertained Philip II with his stories, ended by making a spectacle for Philip III with his exhumed bones.

The file against Román Ramírez, which had led to this sentence, consisted of documents pertaining to a number of charges which only concern us incidentally here, such as the alleged conjuring of spirits in the case of diabolical possession in the village of Tajaguerce (it was this aspect, probably regarded as most sensational at the time, which gave Alarcón the main strand of the plot of his *comedia*). He was accused of participating in Islamic ceremonies and customs, of having been transported through the air on a magic horse and other fantastic things besides. We will not enter here into the details of these charges, interesting as they are: Caro Baroja relates them with great clarity to the background of the ideas of the time. One aspect of the accusations only concerns us here, and that is that diabolical assistance enabled him to recite long passages from novels of chivalry (and other books) when he did not have the actual text before him but only a blank sheet of paper or a book (perhaps upside down) held clasped in his hand. Here, lost in the midst of the balderdash of the Inquisition's accusations, is a nugget of what the student of comparative oral literature will recognise as being authentic information, for this practice is known elsewhere among public narrators and singers of epic songs.

### Román as reciter of novels of chivalry

Most of those who perform narrative songs or poems do so to a characteristic musical accompaniment, and the musical instrument *as an object* is of importance. But some performers use an object which is not a musical instrument, as for example a staff on which to lean, and which can if necessary be addressed. Another object is a book, not, as might at first sight appear, as containing the text, but as an object to be held in the hands. This type of recitation in Serbo-Croat is called *z kniga*, " out of the book ",[12] and this is the style which Román Ramírez employed.

I am of course not suggesting that there is any genetic relationship between the isolated Morisco prose narrator and the many Yugoslav metrical

[12] I have no direct knowledge of the Yugoslav epic tradition. Besides my obvious dependence on the published work of A. B. Lord, I must also acknowledge my indebtedness to Professor R. Auty and to Mr A. L. Lloyd, both of whom addressed the University of London Seminar on Epic during its working sessions 1965-70. It is to be hoped that the efforts of the chairman of this seminar, Professor A. T. Hatto, to secure the publication of the transactions of the seminar will be successful.

singers. Both, however, do give us evidence of early stages of literary evolution which in most other areas are covered over with many strata of development. The accident of the preservation of Román Ramírez's interrogation tells us that techniques surviving from the epic past of Spain lived on in the prose narratives of the books of chivalry.

### History of the genre of libros de caballería in Spain

Whereas novels of chivalry containing such tales as those of Arthur and the Knights of the Round Table or Tristan and Iseult are in France and England, and elsewhere in Europe, phenomena of the Middle Ages, the vogue for these subjects in Spain does not seem to begin until the fourteenth century, and the peak of interest in them came when they were disseminated in the early fifteenth century thanks to the newly-arrived printing presses. Sometimes the novels published then were medieval texts of much earlier date, as in the case of the *Libro del Cavallero Zifar*, sometimes the novels were free adaptations of older books in other languages, but with many additions, so making the Castilian version to most intents a fresh creation, as in the case of *Tristán de Leonis* (1501). Sometimes the books were original works written for the first time in Castilian, as was the case with the second part of *Tristán de Leonis* published in 1535. Books of all three types aroused great enthusiasm at the beginning and in the middle of the sixteenth century, but Sir Henry Thomas in his authoritative study of the genre *Spanish and Portuguese Romances of Chivalry* states what is the generally accepted view when he says that " towards the end of the sixteenth century the romance of chivalry had clearly outworn its welcome ".[13] *Don Quixote* as a satire of the genre has consequently been seen not as the cause of the decline of the vogue so much as the confirmation of its demise. Edward Glaser,[14] on the other hand, has documented the existence of continuous concern about this type of writing, indicating that novels of chivalry were by no means mere antiquarian curiosities by the time of the publication of *Don Quixote*. What is more, any decline of interest in the genre among the inner circle of writers of fashion at court was not necessarily matched by a corresponding waning of interest in them in the provinces. The career of Román Ramírez is ample proof that in Soria and elsewhere in the provinces most heated arguments and long drawn-out feuding could be aroused by desire to hear tales of this sort. The novel of chivalry was emphatically not moribund on the banks of the Duero in 1595.

We know from *Don Quixote* itself how the novels would be enjoyed, either in private reading in the home of an individual like Alonso Quijano himself, or else in public performances in inns and other such places. Román Ramírez was a professional who put on public performances. He claimed that he

---

[13] Sir H. Thomas, *Spanish and Portuguese Romances of Chivalry*, Cambridge, 1920, p. 178.
[14] E. Glaser, " Nuevos datos sobre la crítica de los libros de caballerías en los siglos XVI y XVII ", *Anuario de Estudios Medievales*, 3, Barcelona, 1966, pp. 393-410.

had " read " before King Philip, but his performances would seem to have
been mainly to small groups in private houses. One of the depositions in the
dossier against him gives a vivid picture. The priest Pedro Diaz de Cara-
bantes told how he and various others (including one Francisco de Medrano)
" had been standing in the street by a notary's signboard " when the head
of the watch (alguacil mayor), Alonso de Roa by name, came up to them
and said:

> Vean vuesas mercedes aquel que está allí baxo, señalando a un hombre
> que estaba cabo otro tablero de escribano a treynta o quarenta pasos
> dellos que tenia una capa parda, que este t[estig]o [i.e. Pedro Diaz de
> Carabantes] no le vio el rostro ni le conosce de nombre mas de el
> dicho alguacil dixo que se llamaba Roman y era vezino de la villa de
> Deza, morisco, y que la noche de antes, hallándose el dicho Román
> en casa de don Antonio del Rio, unos cavalleros que estaban allí
> jugando y folgandose en casa del oydor don Gil Ramirez de Arellano,
> algunos de los que allí estaban que le conocían dixeron al dicho
> Román: " Ca, díganos un pedaço de tal libro de cavallerías " que
> allí le señalaron, y de tal capítulo del, y el dicho Román sacó un papel
> en blanco de la faldriquera/ 101 recto/ e mirando a el como leyendo
> essa escriptura dixo un gran pedaço del libro y capítulo que le seña-
> laron, e que lo mismo hazia si le señalaran essa o parte de la Biblia
> o sagrada escriptura, lo qual confirmaronles los mas de los que allí
> estaban, diziendo algunos que se avian y allado presentes a ello, e
> confirmando todo lo sobrescripto ; que no se acuerda este testigo bien
> cuales de los sobredichos se avian hallado presentes mientras que
> relato todo lo sobredicho, pero se acuerda muy bien este testigo que
> el dicho Alonso de Roa dixo [and he goes on to speak of other matters].

Another deposition in the dossier is that of Licenciado Bonifacio or
Bonifaz, an advocate living in Soria. Román cited him, as he was entitled
to do by Inquisition procedure, as an enemy, and so as a possible hostile
witness. He is not significantly more hostile than many others who gave
testimony, and when he says that Román, like most of the Moriscos of Deza,
only went to communion on their wedding day and when they were on their
deathbeds, he is in all likelihood telling the unvarnished truth. His witness
on Román's performances of novels of chivalry seems likely if anything to
have counted in Román's favour:

> E dixo que este testigo ha oydo muchas vezes leer al dicho Román
> Ramírez libros de cavallerias e capitulos dellos que le han pedido que
> lea y el dicho Roman Ramirez lee de memoria los dichos capitulos
> que le han pedido, tomando para dar forma a lo que lee un papel
> qualquiera que le den, y sabe este t[estig]o que aviendole pedido
> algunos capitulos de algunos libros no los ha leydo en forma derecha
> (?) por dezir no aver leydo los dichos libros e asi que el dicho Ramón
> Ramírez a lo que este t[estig]o entiende e a bisto tan solamente lee
> de memoria los libros que a leydo o escuchado, pero no generalmente,
> e que este t[estigo] nunca fizo escrupulo, ni sospecho cosa mala por
> poder ser cosa natural tener tan gran memoria que puede dezir de
> memoria lo que ha leydo mucho ti[em]po ha. E que asi mesmo sabe
> este testigo que a leydo algunas historias divinas de memoria de las

que el dize aver leydo en tiempo de muchacho e preguntandole este t[estig]o al dicho Roman Ramirez porque tuviese tanta memoria, Respondio el dicho Roman Ramirez que el no lo sabia ni avia tomado para ella ninguna cosa pero que sospechaba que por averse criado en casa de Juan de Luna su aguelo e si mismo christiano nuevo natural del Reyno de Aragon del qual este t[estig]o conocio que era grande herbolario e medico le avia dado alguna cosa para tener tan gran memoria pero que el no lo sabia e que los libros que lee dize averlos leydo o oydo leer en t[iem]pos de mochacho o queste t[estig]o le a visto faltar en muchos de los que a leydo a la letra dellos.

It will be seen that this testimony, by reducing Román's powers to the status of exceptional natural, rather than supernatural, phenomena, was likely to clear Román of the charge of having diabolical assistance, for the wording of the charges proferred was that " the Devil told him what he had to read and for this end he had before him a piece of paper ". Bonifaz seems indeed to have been a very level-headed man ; he did not believe Román in everything because he had caught him out in many lies (he tells us later in his testimony) and he took him not for a truthful man but rather for a boastful braggart.

Certainly there are contradictions between Román's statements as reported by Bonifaz and what we learn about Román's ability to read elsewhere. One would assume from what Bonifaz says that Román had been able to read a little since boyhood, but Román explicitly says elsewhere (f 202) that he had learnt to read about thirty years before (i.e. when he was about thirty) by himself after being taught the letters by a child from an alphabet book. The two conflicting stories may both have been partly true: the learning process appears never to have been really completed, and the childhood beginnings and the effort made in manhood to catch up prompted possibly by his purchase of the Spanish translation of *Dioscorides*, a text useful to him in his practice of herbal medicine, were neither of them crowned with complete success. His undoubted powers of memory, his quick wits and his glib tongue will have helped him in most circumstances to hide his lack of fluency in reading. Amongst literate men the illiterate will often go to extraordinary lengths to hide the "shameful" fact that they cannot read. The Inquisitors quite fairly put him through a literacy test, and asked him to read a passage from a book.

They set as the test a book which he had listed when giving the names of books he had possessed. The whole list is of interest, and I will quote it giving in brackets the identifications and the year(s) of publications extracted from the bibliographical notes provided by González Palencia:

" Ha tenido libros como son:
el dicho de Dioscorides y otros
de caballerias:
*Floranvel* (Florambel de Luna, 1532, 1548)
*Amadís* (*de Gaula*)
*Don Cristalián* (*de España* 1545, 1548)

*Don Olivante de Laura* (1564, by Antonio de Torquemada)
*Primaleón* (Book 2 of *Palmerín de Oliva*, 1563, 1566, 1585)
*Don Duardo* (*Don Duardos*, Book 7 of the Portuguese version of *Palmerín de Oliva*, 1587)
*Don Clarián del Amadís* (Don Clarián de Londalis is Book 3 of *Don Clarín de Londalís* 1524)
*El Caballero del Febo* (1580, 1581)
*Don Rogel de Grecia* (Book 9 of *Amadís de Grecia*, 1536, 1546)
*Don Felis Malo* (either, suggests González Palencia, *Felis Magno*, 1531, of 1549 or *Felix Marte de Hircania*, 1556-1557.)
*Carro de Donas* (translated from the Catalan of Eximenis, 1542)
*Flos Sanctorum* (by Alonso de Villegas, 1578)
*Vidas de Emperadores* (probably Mexía's *Historia Cesárea*, 1545 and frequently reprinted)

Fray Juan de Dueñas (wrote *Espejo de consolación de*
y otros que al presente no se acuerda, *tristes* 1589 or perhaps this is more
todos libros de romance. likely to be his *Confesionario*, 1546)
(f 202)

This is indeed a respectable private collection in a period when books were, if no longer rare commodities, at least not to be found in every house. Román does *not* say that he possessed them all at the time of his trial, only that he had possessed them. Presumably once he had a book in his repertoire, he no longer had need of the printed text.

The text chosen for the test shows us that they must have been thoroughly puzzled by this strange man, for the " libro de romance que estaba en la mesa de la sala " from which he was asked to read was Huarte de San Juan's *Examen de Ingenios*. This vernacular treatise on psychology and allied topics was no doubt the centre of the discussions which took place among those trying to understand the old man's mental state. In the test " leyó un poco en un capítulo dél y no paresçió leer despierta ni claramente ".

When pressed he explained what no doubt he had endeavoured to keep secret :

antes que él supiese leer ni lo hubiese deprendido, sabía ya de memoria los más libros de caballerías de los cuales dichos porque Román Ramírez, padre deste confesante, leía muy bien y muchas veces en presencia deste, y así este confesante iba tomando en la memoria lo que le oía leer, y que después su poco a poco fue este confesante deprendiendo a leer y para sí leía lo que le bastaba para irlo decorando y tomando en la memoria.

He then goes on to explain the mumbo-jumbo of pretending to read from a piece of paper, a trick which had given rise to so many accusations:

Siempre que este confesante leía de memoria, tomaba un papel en la mano o un libro que no fuese el mesmo de que leía, y iba mirando por él, teniendo los ojos puestos en él, sin volver las hojas, y que esto lo hacía por no divertir la memoria y llevar más atención en lo que iba leyendo y diciendo, pero no porque le fuese necesario a éste tener en las manos dicho libro y papel para leer.

Nunca leyó de memoria sin tener papel o libro en la mano ; y también lo hacía esto porque pareçía mal leer de cabeça, sin tener algún libro o papel en las manos, y que de lo que sabe y se acordare al presente leerá tres meses de corrida sin tener papel si cosa delante.

The Inquisitor not unreasonably wished to put to the test this claim to such an enormous repertoire, and decided to have him recite one of the books he had mentioned in his list of books once in his hands: *Don Cristalián de España*. One can imagine that the wily Morisco seized at once upon the fact that this placed him in a dilemma. If he had failed to recite from a text, it could have been taken as proof that without diabolical aid (and the Devil might have been taken to be shy of the Holy Office) he could do nothing. And yet he knew quite well that if they tested him carefully against the text he would indeed fail. Should he reveal his professional secrets ? He decided that he had no alternative:

> Dixo que él quiere decir y revelar el secreto deste negocio y la orden de como leía, cosa que no la ha dicho a ánima viviente ni la pensaba decir ; y que si otra cosa hay en ello mas de lo que dixere, mal fuego le queme ; y que lo que pasa es que este confesante tomaba en la memoria cuantos libros y capítulos tenía el libro de *Don Cristalián* y la sustancia de las aventuras y los nombres de las çiudades, reinos, caballeros y princesas que en dichos libros se contenían, y esto lo encomendaba muy bien a la memoria ; y después, cuando lo recitaba, alargaba y acortaba en las raçones cuanto quería, teniendo siempre cuidado de concluír con la sustancia de las aventuras, de suerte que a todos los que le oían reçitar les parecía que iba muy puntual y que no alteraba nada de las razones y lenguaje de los mesmos libros, e que en efecto de verdad, si alguien fuese mirando por el libro de donde éste reçitaba, vería que, aunque no faltaba en la sustançia de las aventuras ni en los nombres, faltaba en muchas de las razones y añadía otras que no estaban allí escriptas ; y que esto lo puede hacer cualquier persona que tenga buen entendimiento, habilidad y memoria, y que no hay otro misterio en esto ; y que como este confesante començó a cobrar fama de hombre de mucha memoria y a tener cabida con caballeros y señores en razón de entretenerlos con estas lecturas y se lo pagaban o hacían mercedes y le llevaban a saraos de damas y a otros entretenimientos, se dió este confesante más a ello y lo estudiaba con más cuidado.

He has thus been forced to reveal that his recitations were not pure memory. What were they then ? They were improvised narrations of known stories in a known style, but not in a fixed form. That is to say that they varied in the same way that the text of Yugoslav epics vary from one performance to another, or in the way that a performance of the *Poema de Mio Cid* would have varied. Ramón Ramírez was certainly a remarkable memory man, an entertainer not too dissimilar from those memory men who, in the days of the music-hall, would tell members of the audience what horse won the Derby in 1909, as an amusing spectacle ; but he was also possibly one of the last in the long line of narrators in Spain who kept audiences, from kings down to country yokels, entertained with traditional stories recounted in traditional wording, fixed but for ever changing. What was fixed was content, style and vocabulary ; what might change were the actual detailed words:

> E luego reçitó de memoria el capítulo primero del segundo libro de *Don Cristalián*, y el capítulo segundo, refiriendo unas batallas y pareçió ser cuentos de caballerías ; y dixo el dicho Román Ramírez que pudiera alargar aquellas batallas y el cuento dellas cuatro horas y que era mas la traza e inventiva que este confesante tenía que no lo que sabe de memoria de los dichos libros ; y que su señoría podía hacer la experiencia, mandando traer el dicho libro de *Don Cristalián* y viendo por él lo que este reçita de memoria y que así hallaría su señoría que este confesante dice la sustancia de las aventuras, y añade y quita razones como le parece.

Then finally we find this tantalizing statement:

> " Y que este confesante tiene compuesto un libro de caballerías que le intitula *Florisdoro de Greçia*, que le daban treçientos reales por lo que tiene escrito ".

We are told no more. Who had paid this publisher's advance ? Perhaps nobody would admit to patronising a suspected wizard. The amount is quite a substantial one. And how could he *write* it down since he has stated that he could read but not write ? Did he dictate his oral composition to an amanuensis, in which case is there perhaps still extant somewhere a portion of a dictated oral text of a novel of chivalry ? It would seem unlikely that Román would have made up gratuitously a story which could so easily be checked, but there is little hope of *Florisdoro de Grecia* ever turning up. Nevertheless the existence of this novel written by a Morisco adds a new dimension to the Morisco Cidi Hamete Benengeli, and to the *Arabic* novel of chivalry which Cervantes had him translate !

After spending some time assembling the facts about a Ramírez who, with his powers of memory, played an unusual part in the dissemination of novels, one cannot fail at least to mention the somewhat better-known case of a Ramírez who did as much a very few years later for plays. (The name differs by one letter, but we may guess that the variation is without significance.)

In his *Plaza universal de todas ciencias y artes* (Madrid, 1615)[15] Cristóbal Suárez de Figueroa has the following to say in his chapter entitled *De los professores de Memoria*:

> Hallase en Madrid al presente un mancebo grandemente memorioso. Llamase Luis Remirez de Arellano, hijo de nobles padres, y natural de Villaescusa de Haro. Este toma de memoria una comedia entera de tres vezes que la oye, sin discrepar un punto en traça y versos. Aplica el primer día a la disposicion ; el segundo a la variedad de la composicion ; el tercero a la puntualidad de las coplas. Deste

[15] C. Suárez de Figueroa, *Plaza Universal de todas ciencias y artes*, Madrid, 1615, f. 237 r. I owe this reference to my colleague, Dr A. K. G. Paterson.

modo encomienda a la memoria las comedias que quiere. En particular tomó assi la Dama Boba, el Principe Perfeto, y la Arcadia, sin
otras. Estando yo oyendo la del Galan de la Membrilla que represen-
tava Sanchez, commençò este autor a cortar el argumento y a inter-
rupir el razonado, tan al descubierto, que obligó le preguntassen de
que procedia somejante aceleracion y truncamiento ; y respondió
publicamente, que estar delante (y señalole) quien en tres dias tomava
de memoria qualquier comedia, y que de temor no les usurpasse
aquella, la recitava tan mal. Alborotose con esto todo el teatro, y
pidieron todos hiziesse pausa, y en fin hasta que salio del Luis Remirez,
on huvo remedio de que se passase delante.

I do not think we should take too seriously the statement that this
Remírez/Ramírez de Arellano was the son of noble parents. We must
remember that in the year 1609-1611 the expulsion of the Moriscos took
place. If a Morisco wished to stay on illegally he had to find some cover.
A name like Ramírez de Arellano could mean only one of two things—either
noble blood or else the status of recent convert—*nuevo convertido*. Hurtado
de Mendoza would be the name of the former viceregal dynasty in Granada,
or else of the Moriscos who adopted the name at baptism. (There was a
similar practice in the United States, where slaves not infrequently adopted
their masters' names, hence the revulsion in recent years against " slave
names " and the invention of exotic substitutes.) If one were a Remírez/
Ramírez in Spain after the expulsion, then one would be forced to claim
that one had such a name by long right and not by recent adoption. I think
it likely that this talented pirate of *comedias* was another Morisco. It is
tempting to speculate whether he might have been a member of the same
Morisco line, even perhaps a son of our Román, although I have absolutely
no evidence to back up this speculation, apart from the similarity of name
and occupation. One would expect Román's family to have changed their
place of residence from Deza after the great scandal there.

*Conclusion*

Román Ramírez was obviously an exceptional and peculiar person.
Generalisations based on his life are likely to be misleading, but his trial
does give us access to information on a stratum of performers of literature
of entertainment of which we had not previously been aware. If there were
other such entertainers (and not necessarily Moriscos), then our puzzlement
with regard to the bewildering textual complexity of early fifteenth century
vernacular texts in Spain may well disappear. The *Abencerraje* story would
have been a story likely to fascinate Román or his father, and if they, on
the basis of a text acquired in manuscript, or indeed in print, had " read "
it carefully, and if this performed version had been set down in writing, then
the sort of variations within a tradition which we find are readily compre-
hensible.

At all events it is now clearly established that the genre of the novel of
chivalry could circulate in the absence of any written text. Far from there

being a clear line of demarcation between popular oral literature of the Middle Ages and the printed book, the product of individual creation after the Renascence, in this case it proves to be extremely difficult to say where oral phenomena end and personal creation in writing takes over. In this, as in so many other things, sixteenth-century Spanish culture emerges as a bewildering mixture of elements which we have since come to judge as incompatible. *Don Quixote* was in a certain sense the first European novel. It makes sense to look at it as a powerful act of individual creation, but it is also helpful to remind ourselves that it was deeply rooted in an established and truly popular oral tradition of entertainment.

L. P. HARVEY

*Queen Mary College, London*

# PUSHKIN IN THE RUSSIAN FOLK-PLAYS

In view of the strong links which have always existed between Russia's oral and written culture, it is perhaps surprising that more attention has not been paid by scholars of Russian literature in the West to the influence of folk-literature and music upon the work of Russian writers. The themes and stylistic features of the epic, the fairy-tale and lyrical song are already strikingly apparent in one of the earliest of Russia's literary masterpieces, the 12th century *Slovo o Polku Igoreve* (*The Lay of Igor' 's Host*) and from then onwards there have been few writers of note in Russia who have not to some extent revealed their awareness of and closeness to this particular aspect of their literary heritage. In the 19th century among the major writers who drew inspiration, each in his own way, from the oral tradition, were Zhukovskii, Pushkin, Kol'tsov, Lermontov, Gogol', Nekrasov and Tolstoy to mention only a few. Pushkin in particular, not only showed his knowledge of and love for Russian folklore in many of his own works but was also an enthusiastic collector of fairy-tales, proverbs and folk-songs. Indeed, in the 1830's he was closely involved in the preparation of the first truly scholarly collection of Russian folk-songs then being compiled by the folklorist P. V. Kireevskii.

The passing of themes and artistic forms between the oral and the written tradition was not, however, merely a one-way process. From the latter half of the 18th century many poems of literary origin which had gained widespread popularity among the folk through the medium of the chapbooks were gradually assimilated into the repertoire of folk-song. The influence of written poetry upon the creators of folk-literature can also be seen in the Russian folk-plays such as *Tsar' Maksimilian*[1] and *Lodka* (*The Ship*).[2] In variants of these plays we find quotations from poems by Ogarev, Glinka and Grebenka, from Zhukovskii's *Svetlana*, Lermontov's *Uznik* (*The Captive*), *Son* (*The Dream*) and *Demon* (*The Demon*), from Pushkin's *Chernaya Shal'* (*The Black Shawl*), *Voron* (*The Raven*), *Brat'ya Razboiniki* (*The Robber Brothers*) and *Gusar* (*The Hussar*).

Such literary borrowings were used basically to enhance the artistic and dramatic impact of the plays. From them came new characters, new situations or a new emphasis to long established parts of the plot and a new emotional and verbal richness to the somewhat naive language of the folk-

---

[1] This was the most widespread and popular of the Russian folk-plays. It describes the martyrdom of the Christian prince Adol'f at the hands of his pagan father, the Tsar' Maksimilian. The martyrdom was followed by a series of duels between the royal champion Anika and a variety of hostile knights. The serious action alternated with comic interludes involving a gravedigger and a doctor.

[2] This play was originally a dramatised version of the 18th century song *Vniz po matushke po Volge* (*Down the river Volga*). It was about the adventures of a band of robbers who plied the Volga in search of booty.

text. Pushkin's hussar and his robber brothers, for instance, both entered the plot of *Tsar' Maksimilian* and *Lodka* respectively as new characters.

Poems of this type were not, however, quoted verbatim in the folk-plays but suffered, as it were, a " sea-change ". Both *Gusar*[3] and *Brat'ya Razboiniki*[4] are good examples of the use made of literary borrowings in the folk-plays and both also clearly reflect the inevitable changes suffered by a piece of literature when it is removed from its "intellectual" surroundings and plunged into a folk medium. Short excerpts from *Gusar* appear in several variants of *Tsar' Maksimilian* but the larger extracts examined here occur in texts published by V. Kostin[5] and E. V. Pomerantseva[6] respectively. *Brat'ya Razboiniki* is quoted twice, almost in full, in the play *Shlyupka (The Boat)*, collected and published by N. E. Onchukov.[7]

Through time these literary quotations, like the texts of the plays themselves, became distorted in various ways. There were a number of reasons for these changes, among them the exigencies of the oral tradition.

One of the characteristic features of oral literature in general is the superstitious attention paid to the exact repetition of a particular action or to the exact reproduction of a fixed part of the text and we know that the Russian folk-actors, like other creators of folk-literature, also had a keen sense of tradition. I. S. Abramov, in his introduction to one variant of *Tsar' Maksimilian*,[8] underlined this characteristic. He observed that most of the actors, especially those playing a " serious " role, were required to have their part completely by heart. Alterations to the text were not allowed. Improvisation was permitted only in the case of the comic characters. Such a rigid attitude towards a text transmitted orally from one generation to the next led to many strange distortions in the texts of the folk-plays and in the songs and poems quoted there. Thus, in the extract from Pushkin's *Brat'ya Razboiniki* as it appears in the play *Shlyupka*[9] the phrase " greshnaya molitva " (" a sinful prayer ") of the original (line 226) has become " grustnaya molitva " (" a sorrowful prayer "). A more serious distortion occurs in *Gusar* in Pomerantseva's text. Here, the actor has confused two meanings of the word *dukh*. In Pushkin, we find the expression *dukhom* (at

---

[3] *The Hussar* is the tale of a Russian soldier billeted near Kiev who takes his widowed landlady as his mistress. One night he discovers she is a witch ; he watches her get up, undress, sip a magic potion and fly up the chimney on a broomstick. He follows her and finds himself at a witches' Sabbath.

[4] A poem about two poor brothers who turn in desperation to highway robbery. They are captured and imprisoned but escape. They swim to safety across a fierce river but one brother dies after his ordeal.

[5] V. Kostin, " K istorii narodnogo teatra: *Tsar' Maksimilian* ", *Etnograficheskoe obozrenie*, Book 37, No. 2 (Moscow 1898), pp. 107-8.

[6] " *Tsar' Maksimilian* ", E. V. Pomerantseva, *Pesni i skazki yaroslavskoi oblasti* (Yaroslavl' 1958), pp. 123-125.

[7] N. E. Onchukov, *Severnye narodnye dramy*, (SPb. 1911), pp. 71-72 and pp. 78-81.

[8] I. S. Abramov, " *Tsar' Maksimilian*: svyatochnaya kumediya ", (SPb. 1904), p. 2. (Offprint from *Izvestiya obshchestva russkogo yazyka i slovesnosti*, Vol. IX, book 3, [1904]).

[9] N. E. Onchukov, op. cit., p. 81.

a gulp), in the play the vulgar use of *dukh* to mean a stink/stench. So Pushkin's stylistically neutral line 78-79, " I dukhom vsyu sklyanku vypil " (" I
drank the whole phial at a gulp ") has turned into the linguistically cruder
" nanyukhalis' my etogo proklyatogo dukha " (" we got a noseful of the
cursed stink ").[10]

The actor's memory was not infallible either ; some stanzas were forgotten and omitted altogether or rendered in approximate prose form. In
the quotation from *Gusar* in Pomerantseva's text stanzas 4-6 and 8-11 of
the original have all been left out as well as the last stanza and considerable
portions of 26, 27 and 28. Some omissions, however, were not simply due
to forgetfulness but to a definite wish to simplify the text, to cut out non-
essentials, particularly lyrical digressions, which might slow down the action.
Therefore, in the plays we are faced not simply with a literary recitation
but with a poem being used and adapted for a specific purpose. In the
second of the two excerpts from *Brat'ya Razboiniki* in *Shlyupka*, for example,
Pushkin's lyrical description of the robber camp on the banks of the Volga
is omitted and the colourful details of the brigands reduced to a single
condensed line, " Zhid, Kalmyk, Bashkir, Tsygan, brat i ya " (" A Jew, a
Kalmyk, a Bashkir, a gypsy, my brother and I ").[11] Similarly omitted are
the somewhat sentimental episode in the poem (lines 116-143) about the
murder of an old man and the subsequent remorse of the assassins ; the
brothers' first reactions to prison life given at length in the poem (lines 157-
174 approx.) have been reduced to a laconic " Togda sil'nei vzyala toska po
prezhnei dole" ("Then longing for our former life returned with doubled
force ") ; the death scene of the younger brother (lines 208-221) is reduced
to bare essentials in the play:—

> " Tri dnya bol'noi ne govoril,
> A na chetvertyi den' pozval menya,
> Pozhal mne ruku,
> Ruka zadrogla; on vzdokhnul
> I na grudi moei usnul."[12]

(" For three days the sick man did not speak,
But on the fourth day he called me,
Squeezed my hand,
His hand trembled, he gave a sigh,
And fell asleep [i.e. died] upon my breast.")

The poem as it appears in this version, stripped of most of its lyrical and
emotional overtones, fits in better with the rougher nature of the robbers
in the folk-play and with the simple, episodic plot. It is also more suitable
in this shortened form for its new dramatic role within the play ; it appears
as a soliloquy in which Pushkin's nameless robber brother has turned into
Egor', a stranger caught wandering in the forest near the robbers' camp and
forced to give an account of himself by their leader.

[10] E. V. Pomerantseva, op. cit., p. 124.
[11] N. E. Onchukov, op. cit., p. 78.
[12] Ibid., p. 80.

When the folk-actor does not remember the original version in full he improvises, substituting for the poet's carefully controlled balance of literary and "folk" style his own more earthy choice of vocabulary. In Pomerant-seva's text of *Gusar* Pushkin's verb *podruzhit'sya* (line 29) (to make friends with) has been substituted with the more vulgar yet more vivid *smignut'sya* (to wink in token of agreement or collusion) ; so Pushkin's line " Ya s nei podruzhilsya " (" I made friends with her ") acquires a coarser meaning in the play. When Pushkins' hussar catches his mistress at the Witches' Sabbath he is not given a chance to speak his mind properly but in the play he shouts rudely " Akh ty baba, akh ty dura, al' na tebe dvoinaya shkura? "[13] All three words *baba* (married peasant woman), *dura* (fool) and *shkura* (skin/ hide) are used in a highly derogatory sense here.

When improvising the narrator tends to expand the original text, draw-ing on the fund of folk constructions and expressions which come readily to mind. Often he makes use of the various types of repetition and the taut-ological devices typical of folk-literature. If one compares certain quotations from *Brat'ya Razboiniki* with their folklorised equivalents one can readily see the sort of expansion which has taken place:—

|  *Pushkin* | *from " Shlyupka "*[14] |
|---|---|
| (line 70) | |
| (*a*) " Vse nashe. Vse sebe *berem*." | (*a*) " *Oborvem, obderem*, vse eto delo nashe." |
| (" It's all ours ! We *take* it all for ourselves.") | (" *We rob them, we fleece them*, That's the trade we're in.") |
| (line 77) | |
| (*b*) " *Tuda* ! K vorotam, i *stuchim*." | (*b*) " *Tuda katim, tuda letim, smelo pospevaem ; stuchim, gremin . . .*" |
| (" *Off we go* ! Up to the gates, and *we knock*.") | (" *Off we gallop, off we fly*, As fast as we can go, *We knock, we make a din . . .*") |
| (line 43) | |
| (*c*) ". . . nashu mladost' *Vskormila* chuzhdaya sem'ya " | (*c*) " *Poila—kormila* nas chuzhaya sem'ya " |
| (" In our youth we were brought up [lit. *fed*] by a strange family.") | (" We were *given food and drink* by a strange family.") |
| (line 74) | |
| (*d*) " Letim *nad snezhnoi glubinoi* " | (*d*) ". . . tuda katim ; *Ne dorogoi, storonoi Pod snezhnoyu glubinoi.*" |
| (" We fly *across the deep snow*.") | (". . . we gallop there ; *Not by the road, by a roundabout way Beneath the snowy depths* [i.e. of the sky].") |

[13] E. V. Pomerantseva, op. cit., p. 125.
[14] N. E. Onchukov, op. cit., pp. 71 and 78.

In the last example the single line describing the robbers dashing over snow in a *troika* has been expanded by the addition of a phrase " Ne dorogoi, storonoi " which is strongly reminiscent of the peasant saying " Lyudi dorogoi, a chort storonoi " (" People go by the road, but the devil takes a roundabout way "), which underlines the evil nature of the robbers' activities.

Repetitions of words and lines not found in the original text and a tendency, common in folk-literature to arrange actions or linguistic units in groups of three, are frequently found in the plays. Pushkin's hussar examines the potion with which Marus'ka, his mistress, turns herself into a witch (line 65):—" Ponyukhal, kislo ! Chto za dryan' ! " (" I sniffed, sour ! What trash ! ") In the folk-play this line is expanded into:—" Nyukhnul—kislo, liznul—ochen' gor'ko, T'fu ty, chert voz'mi, i yad, ne obozhrat'sya by ")[15] (" I took a sniff—sour, I licked it—very bitter, Phew, devil take it, like poison, you couldn't stuff yourself with it ! ")

Numerous details added to Pushkin's texts by the actors have also been borrowed from folk-literature. Constant epithets have been introduced, such as *chastye zvezdy* (thickly clustered stars) in the Pomerantseva text (p. 124) ; in both the Kostin and Pomerantseva variants (pp. 108 and 125 respectively), the hussar's horse is described as *kon' voronoi* (black horse), the constant epithet again being an addition. The magical numbers three and seven, constantly recurring in folklore, make an appearance too. As a result, the simple *svechka* (candle) in Pushkin (lines 53—54) becomes "tri sal'nye svechki " (" three tallow candles "). Similarly, in place of " Pod lavkoi dremlet kot " (" under a bench the cat dozes "), there appears " Lezhit kot, Tomu sem'desyat sem' let " (" Lying there is the cat, which is seventy-seven years old ".[16]

Interesting changes can also be observed in the metrical and rhyme structure of Pushkin's poems. Where the actor has forgotten the exact lines but not necessarily the general content he automatically remakes the verses on the pattern of folk-verse, *raeshnyi stikh*. This was a verse form to be found in many types of popular literature in the 18th century, the period of genesis of both *Lodka* and *Tsar' Maksimilian*. Its rhythm was derived not from a regular alternation of stressed and unstressed syllables, but from the groups of major stresses (usually 2/3) in each line. There was no rhyme scheme as such but rhyming couplets were common and runs of up to three or four rhyming lines were not infrequent. *Raeshnyi stikh* was so called because of its use in the humorous monologues of the *raeshnyi ded*, the fairground comic or owner of peep-shows known as *raek*.

Changes to this type of verse can be seen in the following extracts from *Gusar* in the Kostin variant of *Tsar' Maksimilian* (pp. 107, 108) where rhyming couplets take the place of Pushkin's ab/ab rhyme scheme and two/

[15] E. V. Pomerantzeva, op. cit., p. 124.
[16] Ibid.

three major stresses per line take the place of his irregular iambic metre:—

(a) " Byvalo napóit, nakórmit,
Da sorkovushku vinstá prigotóvit."
(" She saw I had plenty to eat and drink,
She'd bring out a bottle of wine for me.")

(b) " Tý postrél
Zachem cyudá pospél ? "
(" What are you doing here, you bold rascal ? ")

(c) " Kák, ya gusar prisyázhnyi
Da poédu tebe na kochergé gryáznoi."
(" How can you expect me, a cavalry hussar,
To mount a dirty poker.")

There are also examples of *raeshnyi stikh* in *Gusar* from Pomerantseva's text of *Tsar' Maksimilian* (p. 125) such as:—

" Shéya dugói,
Gríva volnói,
Khvóst krasnoperekópskoyu trubói."
(" Its neck arched like a bow,
Its mane like a wave,
Its tail like a horn of Jericho.")

Incidentally, this expanded version of Pushkin's line 104 incorporates a peculiarly distorted metaphor. The Russian expression " a tail like a horn " (*truba*) to describe a particularly bushy horse's tail has been combined with the expression " a horn of Jericho " (misspelt) which usually indicates a very loud voice.

Again, in Kostin's text (p. 108) the folk-actor has not been able to resist adding a fifth line to one of Pushkin's four line stanzas (stanza 22 in *Gusar*) rhyming ab/ab, thus creating a final rhyming couplet on the pattern of *raeshnyi stikh*:—

" Glyazhu-gora ; na toi gore,
Kipyat kotly, poyut, igrayut,
Svistyat i v merzostnoi igre
Zhida s lyagushkoyu venchayut,
Da moyu Marús'ku zabalýayut."
(" I look up—and there's a mountain ;
On the mountain,
Cauldrons bubble, people sing, play,
Whistle and in a loathsome game
Marry a Jew off to a frog,
They're entertaining my Marus'ka.")

There are many examples of *raeshnyi stikh* in *Brat'ya Razboiniki* too from Onchukov's text (pp. 78-79) as for example:—

" Tudá stremímsya,
Tám stuchímsya,
K sebe khozýaiku vyzyvaem, p'em gulýaem,
K sebe krasnykh dévushek laskáem."
(" We gallop towards the place,
We knock,
Call out the lady of the house, drink, have a good time,
Make up to the pretty girls.")

The assimilation of these poems into a folk-text which was at the same time a dramatic work brought in its wake another series of changes. Pushkin's hussar, for instance, became an accepted character in the folk-play and appears in his own right in variants where Pushkin's poem is not quoted at all.

The presence of an audience has had an obvious effect upon the structure of the quoted poems. In the Pomerantseva variant (p. 123) the hussar, upon entering the acting arena, prefaces his tale with an address to his audience in the style of the fairground clowns (*balagannye dedy*):—

" Zdravstvuite gospoda,
Vtoroi raz zayavlyayus' k vam syuda,
Vtoroi raz prikhozhu
I ochen' vam interesno rasskazhu."
(" Hello there, ladies and gentlemen,
For the second time I stand before you,
For the second time I have come to you
And I am going to tell you a very interesting story.")

Again, in the play *Shlyupka* (p. 71), the robber narrating the poem addresses his audience directly. Just before he tells how he and his brother were captured he turns to them and says:—

" No i tut, ne dolgo, druz'ya, popirovali . . ."
(" But, friends, this gay life didn't last for long . . .")

The ready assimilation of these two long poems into the oral tradition is perhaps less surprising when one remembers that both were in any case themselves influenced by popular and oral literature. Pushkin based his *Brat'ya Razboiniki* on a real incident which had come to his attention while he was living at Ekaterinoslav but at the time of writing the poem, which was to have been part of a much longer work about the life of a robber-band, he was familiarising himself with all types of literature upon this theme, including folk legends.

The writing of *Gusar* in 1833, at a time when Pushkin was keenly interested in folk-literature, was probably inspired by the publication in 1833 of the short story *Kievskie ved'my* by Somov which appeared in the same anthology as Pushkin's story *Domik v Kolomne*. Somov's tale was itself based on the many Ukrainian legends about the witch and the soldier and it is clear that Pushkin also was familiar with this type of literature. There are several incidents in Pushkin's poem which do not occur in Somov's story but which do appear in some versions of the folk-tales.[17]

                                        ELIZABETH A. WARNER
*Hull*

---

[17] For further details see P. Bogatyrev, " Stikhotvorenie Pushkina *Gusar* ", *Ocherki po poetike Pushkina* (Berlin 1923).